D0095874

FOLLOW ME DOWN TO
DUBLIN

FOLLOW ME DOWN TO
DUBLIN

The City Through the Voices of Its People

DEIRDRE
PURCELL

HACHETTE
BOOKS
IRELAND

First published in 2007 by Hodder Headline Ireland
First published in paperback 2009 by Hachette Books Ireland

1

A CIP catalogue record for this title is available from the British
Library.

ISBN 978 0 340 99287 6

Typeset in Sabon 11pt by Sin É Design
Cover and interior design by Sin É Design
Printed and bound by Clays Limited, St. Ives plc

Hachette Books Irelands policy is to use papers that are natural,
renewable and recyclable products and made from wood grown in
sustainable forests. The logging and manufacturing processes are
expected to conform to the environmental regulations of the
country of origin.

Hachette Books Ireland
8 Castlecourt Centre
Castleknock
Dublin 15, Ireland

A division of Hachette UK Ltd,
338 Euston Road, London NW1 3BH, England

www.hbgi.ie

Contents

This book is dedicated to Adrian, Simon, Caroline, Justin and Zoë; this is how it was.

Introduction

One, two, three, O'Leary,
Four, five, six O'Leary,
Seven, eight, nine, O'Leary,
Ten O'Leary, catch the ball.

I don't know who O'Leary was, but still at the oddest times, the tune to this rhyme, chanted as we Dub children juggled rubber balls against a convenient wall, sounds like a comforting mantra in my ears.

Although many other tunes continue to bubble like spring water into the muddy pool of my life, my hope for this book is that, while describing days gone by and prompting memories, it will also elicit a sense of a changed and changing capital. There are twenty-one voices here, my own and those of twenty other individuals. We have all experienced Dublin's transformation, but while many spoke of the accelerated pace of physical change to the infrastructure of their city, nobody mourned modernisation except to note the concomitant loss of 'community'. Proof that buildings are not as important as people – but this is not to be a 'Rare Old Times' book.

Although recollection tends to soften experience and inevitably, much of our collective memory is happy, it is important to acknowledge that for many of our fellow citizens there was a great deal of hardship, poverty and illness. The TB, psychiatric and fever hospitals were full. Polio victims limped in their callipers, the belt and cane were wielded with enthusiastic savagery in the schools and Archbishop John McQuaid exerted what seemed sometimes to be supreme authority over the lives and loves of Dubliners.

Emigration was a fact of life, as was mass movement from Dublin's seething core to the fields of Finglas, Crumlin, Ballymun and other margins of the city. In current terms, the writer Ronan Sheehan has a singular take on this displacement, replicated at present in the dash to new estates in Meath, Kildare, Louth, Westmeath, Laois, Offaly and Wexford. While many people believe, he says, that to move away from their place of birth is to climb a property ladder, in doing so they immediately become the New Dispossessed.

The children at Dublin's heart had no notion of this, of course, when they were moved from cramped and unsanitary flats to the windy fields and heights. In any event, they were still within a bus ride of O'Connell Street. This was a time when children, like myself from the age of five, were thought safely capable not only of playing free of adult supervision, but of travelling alone to the city centre. So even as mothers dug horse dung into the rubbled 'soil' of front gardens to plant borders of sweet williams, antirrhinums, Michaelmas daisies and wallflowers, the offspring swarmed, ant-like, over the half-made roads and avenues to colonise them for street games.

Adults made the most of leisure. In the decades under consideration – the forties, fifties, sixties and early seventies (into the eighties for some) – a few bottles of stout and ham sandwiches were sufficient to ensure a jolly gathering with well-rehearsed party pieces. 'The outdoors' was huge, catered for with Guiding, Scouting, An Óige hostelling or just plain rambling. In the forties, groups banded together in 'milk clubs', which biked off on outings, stopped somewhere to quench their thirst with a bottle of the white stuff, then set off for home again. My parents once cycled to Cullohill in Co. Laois, to attend a dance.

The city's cinemas, dance-halls and variety theatres thrived, while the Phoenix Park, St Stephen's Green and Collinstown airport – for watching the planes and, later on, riding the escalators – were open and free to all, as was the occasional street theatre offered by famous visitors. Thirty thousand people thronged O'Connell Street to catch a glimpse of Princess Grace of Monaco and her husband, Prince Rainier. So great was that crush that fourteen people were sent to hospital and there were fifty minor injuries.

Some of our visitors were visibly bemused at their reception: on emerging through the doorway of his aircraft, Bob Hope seemed startled by the bagpipe skirl of the Emerald Girls Pipe Band. And God knows what Louis Armstrong thought on being researched for a *Late Late Show* appearance by a fledgling journalist named Vincent

Browne, whose interests, even then, lay in areas other than trumpet players or celebrity. Having run out of prepared questions, Browne found himself blurting: 'How come you have such white teeth?'

And during John and Jackie Kennedy's visit in June 1963, the thirty-fifth US president and his wife must have wondered why we were shooting rolls of bus-tickets at their limousine. Any one of us could have told him it was our peculiarly Dublin version of tickertape. The acquisition of bus roll was something to which we all aspired. Every time a bus pulled into a stop, whether in Ballymun, where I lived, or in O'Connell Street, the conductor, battened into his niche on the open platform, was confronted by several beseeching urchins: 'Any rolls, Mister? Mister! Mister! Any rolls?'

The Rolling Stones (no pun intended!) came and went, as did the Beatles, Cliff Richard and Roy Rogers with Dale and Trigger. In 1966, Bing Crosby arrived to shoot a Christmas special for American TV. That happened during my time at the Abbey Theatre and I was in the stalls while he and his crew used our stage to shoot a sequence. Between takes, the icon showed his businessman's teeth, tapping his feet impatiently while microphones picked up his muttering: 'Come on, come on – time is money . . . '

For a few, the universities were gates to a wider world: in the memory of Karen Erwin, Trinity College was a walled oasis of liberal learning in the heart of the city. And everyone, rich and poor, thronged to the famous department stores and smaller shops of Dublin – Frawleys, Guineys, Clerys, Arnotts,

Pyms, Bests, McBirneys and Switzers – staffed with professionally trained and courteous assistants. The intricately tiled Findlaters on O'Connell Street was worth a visit if only for the smells – of different teas, salty bacon fresh baking.

Some of my gallant twenty did define the city by its smells: pleasant – hops, bakeries and grain delivery lorries – or horrid – the Liffey at low tide, the stench from the abattoirs and the 'alcoholicky' pong from the bonded wine cellars near the Seville Place home of the writer and filmmaker Peter Sheridan. Butchers, such as Caffreys and Donohoes in Moore Street, were filled with displays of hearts, livers, kidneys, tripe, pigs' cheeks; along with its fish, Hanlons carried in its window a macabre hanging row of rabbits' furry bodies, until myxomatosis. This wheel, at least, has turned full circle.

Many recalled their fathers tending vegetable and flower allotments, or full city farms created in back gardens. Alongside his hen run, a neighbour of the Finglas poet Dermot Bolger even created a football field, complete with specialised pitch soakage so rain would not stop play. The family of broadcaster Catherine Hogan made use of a grassy acre on the roofs of adjoining warehouses in Power's Distillery on Thomas Street to grow rhubarb.

The streets of the new city suburbs rang with the cries of van men selling vegetables, meat, bread, milk and Friday fish: herring, whiting, ray wing, whelks, cockles and periwinkles – plaice if you were flush that week. The slops man collected pig swill in two barrels balanced perilously on his horse-drawn cart, the wheezing and black-faced coalman rang a handbell for attention and, if you answered his summons, emptied his hundredweight sacks directly into the shed in your back garden. The rag-and-bone man paid for what you gave him with jam-jars, which your mother immediately scalded to hold jam and jelly made from blackberries and crab apples gathered from hedgerows on the country roads just a walk away.

The make-do-and-mend domestic skill of the average person was extraordinary in a city that ran on thrift. As well as tilling the gardens, our fathers could mend shoes as well as bicycle punctures. My mother sliced off the bottoms of my father's shirts to make new collars; my own clothes were cut from hers and my aunts', with a doorstep hem left so the garment could be lengthened as I grew.

Shops would take a deposit on any item. My two interviewees from Frawleys, Geraldine Kelly and Liam Hayden, speak of tripping over the 'put by' mounds of already wrapped parcels. Frank O'Dea of Bests Menswear sold shirts with two detachable collars – and some with Magic Cuffs: when the first pair got dirty, you merely pulled down a second. And when the Peter Mark hairdressing chain set up a salon in the ILAC Centre shopping mall alongside Moore Street, stallholders were known to pay for haircuts with bags of apples.

Discontent was not the dominant driver it is today and very few, as far as I can judge, felt hard done by when a pennyworth of 'broken biscuits' was a treat for any chiseller and when a box of coloured chalk and a slate, or crayons and a colouring book were major presents in a Christmas stocking.

Cars and telephones were serious luxuries, but we took for granted that letters posted in the morning in one Dublin district were delivered in another that afternoon, that bicycles were plentiful and good value if bought second-hand, that bus fares would remain cheap and the buses themselves relatively untrammelled in their smoky progress.

Small-scale saving was standard – in Christmas clubs run by local shops, in post office books, even in old tea canisters kept on a high kitchen shelf. As a result, many families could rise to the cost of a fortnight in Butlin's, or a holiday rental in Rush or Skerries, even to travel to the Isle of Man for a few days on the steam packet docked near Butt Bridge. And if, one year, you couldn't afford it, well, that was life and there was always next summer. In the meantime you could take a bus to Dollymount beach or Clontarf baths, or a train to the baths in Dun Laoghaire and Blackrock. Or pack a picnic for The Bots: the National Botanical Gardens in Glasnevin.

Again, it has to be remembered that these cheerful observations are stalked by the long, sinister shadows of reformatories, intolerance, repression and fear. Dubliners, though, are resilient.

I do remember squalor, but not graffiti or gratuitous violence. I remember drunks but not mayhem. I remember affection for individual eccentricities such as the balletic choreography of the beautiful woman, fashionably dressed with hair in a chignon, who was a fixture at the O'Connell

Street crossing between Henry and North Earl Streets as she tried to pull Dublin back under the mantle of Our Lady by waving a rosary. I remember the ritual of the Seven Churches on Holy Thursday (but memory failed me in recalling exactly which seven).

And I remember in the eighties interviewing (for the *Sunday Tribune*) the grocer and serial entrepreneur Pat Quinn about his new and gorgeously appointed snooker emporium in a neglected quarter of Pearse Street. In his presence, I marvelled aloud at the plush carpeting, top-notch tables, expensive seating and lighting. 'How are you going to ensure that it will stay this way and won't be trashed?'

I have never forgotten the essence of his quiet reply: 'Give people quality, they'll respect it; give them rubbish, they'll rubbish it.' Although in the long term his snooker hall did not survive for economic reasons, he was proven right.

When I began to write fiction, my first London editor had great difficulty in accepting some of the plot points in my novels where I deemed it perfectly natural that a character strolling along O'Connell Street should by chance run into a pal she hadn't seen for many years. Such coincidences, she insisted, were unbelievable within a large modern city, a capital city.

Of course, any Dubliner will tell you that they are not. I have seldom walked through the streets of Dublin without encountering at least one friend or acquaintance. It is a living function of what one of the interviewees here, Aidan Mathews, refers to as the polity, a city of ideal size and population as described by Aristotle.

But now that 'Dublin' stretches from Gorey to Dundalk and from the sea to Mullingar, perhaps such encounters will no longer be as frequent as they were.

Deirdre Purcell, 19 August 2007

Suits You Sir . . .

When you ordered a bespoke suit from Bests (It's Best to Be Sure; The Woman in Your Life Knows Best) you were measured with meticulous care by the salesman. These statistics were recorded on your personal docket, which was then sent off, along with the cloth you had chosen, to the company's tailors in Westmoreland Street.

What you did not see was that your docket had been peppered with mysterious yet tactful letter codes about the state of you. If you had had access to it, among other notations, you might have read:

PC – Prominent Chest (a beer belly)

RB – Round Back (a stoop)

VRB – Very Round Back (your basic hump)

The codes were added by the salesman to give the cutter an indication of where to be generous, where to tuck. In other words, how to morph you, Quasimodo, into a lithe Errol Flynn.

Or did you know that at one time Bests employed a cutter from Savile Row? 'He was a man of independent means. Lived in the Gresham. He had great flair.' In this instance, flair comes with experience, and instinct in knowing how to adjust the drape of the fabric before cutting it, then in deciding exactly where and how to wield the tailoring scissors. Louis Copeland Senior, for instance, was regarded within the trade as one of the most gifted tailors in the town and acknowledged as such. By common consent he was also referred to as 'a gent', the true Dub encomium.

I am in Raheny on the northside of Dublin, in Frank and Helen O'Dea's house where a person could safely eat from any surface without using a plate. Through the sitting-room window, the garden is heavy with red roses and in here the tea-tray has been prepared with cream and home-made jam for Helen's home-baked scones. Faced with such standards and in this couple's elegant presence, I feel pretty inadequate.

I should have known. In years gone by the invitation, 'Will you come up to the house?' was always a formal summons and included hospitality. The phrase exuded pride. In my memory, no one who had issued such a call ever apologised for 'the state of the place' as you crossed the threshold.

Frank, spare of frame and with a humorous mouth, speaks with the type of Dublin accent that has almost vanished from our streets, in which syllables are given consideration and a consonant at the end of a word is always heard. He spent most of his working life selling from the floor of Bests in the heart of the city. Along with Burtons on the opposite corner, his shop, at the junction of North Earl Street and O'Connell Street, faced Henry Street and, at Nelson's Pillar, was part of the busiest pedestrian crossing in the country. 'It was one of the premier retail locations in Dublin.'

It still is, but with pedestrianisation and bus lanes it is sometimes hard to remember that at one time cars could park in O'Connell Street 'or in Waterford Street for five shillings a week, or alternatively, you could leave your bike in a basement in Marlborough Street for just a few bob'.

The shop had another huge advantage in that many buses stopped outside it, 'and in the evenings, the bus queues snaked all down North Earl Street and around the back of Clerys'. This afforded plenty of opportunity to tempt potential customers as, in enforced stasis, they whailed away their time in the queues by viewing the nearby shop windows. 'Bests always concentrated on its displays and we made a very large proportion of our sales that way. People came in: "I want that shirt, or tie, or jumper that's in the window."'

Ties, white collars and hankies for Christmas 'and every man in Dublin seemed to get a present of at least one new shirt'. Your tie, of course, was always in demand and was the standard quick-seller at tea-time, when any mickey-dazzler who wanted to impress a woman that night could dash in off the bus, buy a new one and be back on board before the last person in the queue had found a seat. No one had much money then so the purchase of a new tie, sometimes secured with a proper knot round the customer's neck by an obliging member of Bests' staff, would demonstrate that An Effort had been made.

All over Dublin in the first half of the last century, the clothing trade was populated and run by skilled Jewish families, Sabins, for instance, or Newmans, who traded as Premier Tailors; a company called Maxwell Cliffords were on the Bests site before Bests itself was established in 1948. It was relatively small then, beside Goggins, a little huckster's shop, with Barrons, a pram and cot shop trading in the upstairs rooms.

In Frank's time, a new pair of gloves or a hat was not carelessly acquired but a considered purchase, while shirts, always boxed, were frequently presented with two collars, collar studs and cufflinks.

Self-service was unknown. Instead, assistants stood behind gleaming counters, waiting to make eye-contact with a cus- tomer, who was valued not only as a conduit to commission, or repeat business, but also because that was what each had been trained to do. Menswear retail was a good stready job; its quali- fied staff carried a measuring tape, scissors and tailor's chalk at all times, and if you wanted to earn that privilege, you had first to enter an apprenticeship.

'Arnotts, for instance, would have had hundreds of apprentices. You did your time for three years, and for the first three months, your tools were a dustpan and a brush! Then, after those three years, you were usually let go but you were so well trained you could get a job. It was eight years before you got the top union wage.'

Helen prompts him on the importance of commission. The rate was threepence in the pound. This was before decimal-isation, so for every 240 pennies you took in from the customer, you earned three for yourself. It was necessary because the basic wage was low. 'In a busy shop you could earn more in commission than you did in your wages.'

Bests was busy. The shop dressed the two most successful showbands in Ireland, the Miami and the Royal, whose members were 'very particular' about their stage suits, hand-made and customised with perhaps a small piece of detailing on a lapel or a breast pocket. 'It was always a big order: six suits, six spares – twelve suits in all – and if they were happy with what they got they'd come back in to get their personal stuff too.' So it was worth going the extra mile and the bands got the red-carpet treatment – albeit through a fug of cigarette smoke. There were ashtrays on every counter and the 'ventilation system' blew air inwards.

The salient point is that Frank O'Dea 'regularly' took home twice his basic wage in commission 'and sometimes even three times as much'. So while the showbands were VVIPs, every customer was a king.

He introduces me to a new word. My own grandmother, who served her time with a tailor, always referred to herself as such, but if she had worked for Bests, she would have been a 'tailoress'. And while the top menswear shops always had alteration hands on the premises as a vital part of the service, Frank felt it unfair that they were paid far less than the men on the sales floor, not least because their skills included the copying of American, and later Italian, suit styles with, in those early years, only pictures from *Esquire* magazine to guide them.

Until 1948, imports to the trade were tightly controlled with 25 per cent duty on ready-mades, and limits on the yardage of 'foreign' cloths, from the mills of England or Italy, that could be imported on licence. In those lean years, when a suit, or a jacket and trousers, was a major purchase, government policy was that home producers had to be supported.

However, the Irish companies, including Murroughs and McGees, produced a limited range and in Frank O'Dea's retrospective assessment, the styles and colours of the fabrics they offered were 'very restricted, very dark, just a few shades of grey or brown'. As a result, a fair bit of unofficial trading went on within the various clothiers. If one firm did not order the full quota on its licence in any one period it would offer the surplus to another, who paid for the privilege with a percentage mark-up agreed across the industry. Menswear was profitable, but it was a business conducted, in general, by gentlemen. (Nowadays this arrangement would probably be called a cartel and would be viewed with suspicion by the Competition Authority.) Margins and mark-ups on clothes were officially controlled too – to 25 per cent. 'If you bought for twenty you had to sell for a maximum of twenty-five. Invoices were inspected. We were never prosecuted. We were too clever.'

Along with their hard-earned money, customers had to present clothing-ration stamps with cash. But, as ever, there were opportunists in search of easy profits, spivs who roamed the city streets offering a pittance in return for the stamps of the poor. In an era when the Herald Boot Fund and the Lord Mayor's Coal Fund were vital for survival, many were desperate for the necessities of life and accepted whatever few pence they were offered by those leeches.

As workers, Frank and his colleagues were rivalrous on the sales floor – a successful sale was known as a 'swap' – but always courteous to each other. They had a communal gripe, though: their shop was always dark, shadowed by the towering granite column of The Pillar a few yards away.

The foundation stone of this landmark, one of the most familiar in the Dublin streetscape, was laid in 1808 to commemorate the battle of Trafalgar. The entrance was underground, but at the beginning of the last century, a porch was added so that generations of visitors – including even a few curious Dubliners like me and my Auntie Nellie – could walk in directly from the street. Its internal circular staircase, polished and made concave by generations of visitors' boots and shoes, seemed never-ending but eventually, panting, you emerged into the cage surrounding Nelson's statue, sculpted by a Corkman, Thomas Kirk, to admire the smoggy, foggy view to the farmlands in the west and south.

Bests' staff, though, wouldn't have minded if the thing was taken out of their sight and, sure enough, on the morning of 8 March 1966, when he was upstairs at home preparing for the workday ahead, Frank heard a shout from Helen, who, preparing his breakfast, had switched on the wireless to listen to the news.

She called up to tell him that the Pillar had been blown up.

'What about the shop?' Frank had his priorities.

'They didn't say anything about the shop.'

He abandoned all but the most necessary ablutions that morning to dash into North Earl Street – and found that while Bests and the area around it had been cordoned off, the IRA had done a professional job. 'Two or three of the windows. That's all. I couldn't believe it. It was easily cleaned up and dealt with and we were open again for business.'

But now the view from their front door and windows was of a huge and very ugly stump.

That couldn't be left there. The Irish Army was called in.

So in they came and the shop windows went up again. Comprehensively this time. All of them and not only in Bests: 'Every window in the vicinity was hammered.'

At some stage during that extraordinary week, Nelson's head was recovered from the rubble and produced on stage during a Dubliners' concert so the crowd could cheer at his downfall. It is now in the Dublin Civic Museum.

There is one other titbit about this episode that I find irresistible. When excavations were taking place to erect the Spire of Dublin on the Pillar's site, there was great excitement when a time capsule was found buried in the original foundations. When it was opened, however, it contained nothing but a list of what was supposed to have been put into it.

This seems to me to be a peculiarly Dublin thing to have done in 1808 to spite the British. I can see an O'Casey Joxer-like character sealing the tantalising note into the empty box, then cementing it in place, all the while assuring his superiors on the site that everything was in order. Next day, there he was, standing in the crowd, hee-heeing privately to himself as he watched the lord lieutenant of Ireland tap-tapping on the foundation stone with his effin' ceremonial trowel.

Before 'outlets' and 'malls', the area immediately around Bests amounted to a self-contained shopping village, where every retail need could be met within a hundred yards. The names represent a diary of my childhood shopping trips with my mother or aunt, and Frank O'Dea remembers them all. Clerys for everything. Burtons, Kingstons, Premier Tailors, Collins or Bests for menswear, Kellys for boyswear, O'Reillys and Bolgers for 'general clothing', Densons or Saxone for shoes.

Ladies were well served at Gleesons and Lorna Ladies, while Madam Nora could supply their more intimate needs with gloves, scarves and handbags. If they could sew, which most could, the ladies could buy their tweeds in O'Beirne and Fitzgibbon, their silks in Cassidys. 'And everybody went to Rowes for their buttons.'

You could get your fresh bread in Downes' bakery, your general groceries in the Home and Colonial, or Maypole, your loose tea from Beckers, your cakes and buns in the

Kilmore. You dried your dishes and dressed your bed in linens from Michael Guineys or Duffys. You decimated your savings from the Munster and Leinster Bank to buy a bauble from Hopkins and Hopkins, McDowells or Jamesons.

And when you were finished shopping, you could go to the Pillar Picture House or the Savoy to watch a film, stretch your legs as far as the Broadway for a mixed grill or a sundae, or even cross to the other side of O'Connell Street for a cup of tea and a fancy at the Monument Creamery Café.

This is just a selection: there were more. Frank's memory is good.

It is hard, I suppose, in this era of plenty and 100 per cent interest-only mortgages, to remember what Dublin was like in the fifties and early sixties. Then, to take a taxi was either a rare treat or the sign of a dire emergency, and it was not uncommon for even people in regular employment to choose between buying a daily newspaper or taking the bus. Then, you put deposits on shop goods such as shoes, and paid off a little more each payday until – oh, happy day! – the last shilling was handed over and the shoes were yours. It took me sixteen weeks to buy my first pair at 37/6d after I started work. I didn't feel it was a penance to wait – because it was the norm.

So it is probably difficult nowadays to envisage the plight of the news vendor outside Bests, who, bundle of papers under his arm, coughed his way up and down the bus queues, growing sicker every day from malnutrition and exposure. When he died, another family member took up the 'business' until he, too, died, then another and another . . .

Frank O'Dea is silent for a moment. Then: 'They all died of TB. All of them.' The modern equivalent are the Nigerians and Congolese who, at traffic-lights in the city and at the entrances to the motorways, walk up and down the queues of rush-hour motorists, displaying the front pages of the *Evening Herald*. At least they have been given all-weather protective clothing.

Frank O'Dea wrote down the following story. It encapsulates not only the work ethic of the service industry in that period, and the pride taken by those working in it, but the endemic thrift of the Dubliner.

A customer came into Bests forty years ago. He wanted a very good dark grey suit, suitable to get married in. I showed the customer and his fiancée our selection of top-quality materials and they duly picked out a very nice charcoal grey suiting. I measured the customer, gave him a fitting two weeks later and had the suit finished for his wedding. The suit looked really good and he was very pleased. I assured him that it was of a very high quality and jokingly said that it would probably last him a lifetime.

He wore the suit for the wedding and for every special occasion afterwards, like family weddings and christenings. He died just over one year ago and was buried in the same charcoal grey suit.

This story is true. The man was my brother.

Café Society

In 1932, at the age of fourteen, my mother was sent to work in the Broadway Café on O'Connell Street, as mentioned by Frank O'Dea. She had no experience of waitressing, obviously, but because she was graceful, elegant and beautiful, it was decided that she could work behind the cake counter just inside the entrance to the shop.

She had never been to Dublin before, but from Durrow where the family lived, word was sent to the policeman on point duty at O'Connell Bridge, a Laois man, famous for the elbow-length white gauntlets he wore, to keep an eye on her: the Broadway was within sight of his patch.

The Laois man took this request literally. Each time he spotted her he stopped traffic 'with a wave of his hand', as the song says, and beckoned her towards him to ascertain if she was being 'treated right' or if she had any problems at all at all. It felt marvellous, she said, to be standing surrounded by packed swarms of cyclists, horse-carts and motor-cars while their impatient riders and drivers waited for her to finish her chat with the man in charge. In her later years, she wrote feature articles and short stories, many of which were published in columns such as 'Petticoat Panel' in the *Evening Press*. She had offered the following piece to a couple of outlets but she was in her seventies, the *Evening Press* was defunct and there was really no place for articles like hers.

Turn the page, Mamma. Because here it is.

Broadway Babies
Maureen Purcell

'Gigli dined in this restaurant,' declared the notice placed outside the door of the Broadway Restaurant and Soda Fountain in Lower O'Connell Street.

In the late thirties and early forties, you pushed open the swing doors and were immediately embraced by scents of cakes, polished oak, the metallic tang of silver appointments and the fresh-air smell of the bleached white linen tablecloths and napkins. White-capped and aproned waitresses sped among the customers; the cash register and my gleaming glass cake counter were to the left. You descended to the Grill Room and the Smoke Room, or ascended to the Tea Lounge, Blue Room and Music Room by means of a beautiful carved and curved staircase. The ballroom was down to the right.

The Broadway's owner was an Italian gentleman, whose notion of propriety forbade staff to use make-up, particularly nail polish – 'pig's blood', as he called it. In fact, he treated us like boarding-school inmates, which was understandable since, from my pitch behind the cakes, I colluded with those who surreptitiously gulped the cream buns, éclairs and meringues for which the restaurant was famous. (And one waitress got round the 'pig's blood' edict by removing the polish from her thumbnails only and, while serving the boss, concealed the others under trays or plates.

In the early forties, during the war, many foreign ships were trapped in Dublin port, and our restaurant, being the upmarket one nearest the port, became a regular haunt for the crews. Many of the officers teamed up with our staff and I have to say that their behaviour was exemplary. My own conquest was Welsh. Although we were serious about one another for a time, he went back to London, signed on with a Merchant Navy ship for a voyage to the West Indies and, on their first day at sea, all aboard were lost to a torpedo.

Not for the first time, I turned to Nora for solace. Serene, motherly and always welcoming, Nora was the resident lady in the Ladies' Refuge Room. She lent an egalitarian shoulder on which all of us, customers and staff, laid our troubles. Nora gave the same ear to the woman who spoke 'posh' and looked for the 'scratchers' to clean the pots and the 'scrubbers' to scrub the back stairs as she did to the seventeen-year-old girl from the country who was a runaway from an arranged marriage to a retired policeman. It was a safe, feminine world of secrets up there on the second floor. Nora's domain even included a cosmetics counter and curling tongs.

The Broadway Tea Lounge Orchestra, led by lady violinist Madame van Ast (with Alfie Barry, an ancestor of the Billy Barry School, on drums) obliged us with requests, any- thing from the *Cavalleria Rusticana's* Intermezzo to 'In the Mood'. We even boasted our own singing waitress, Tiny Greene, an untrained soprano with a wonderful range. She was not paid for her singing: she felt that the applause and the time off from waiting at tables were reward enough.

I had a similar bonus when I was delegated to dance with an Argentinian sailor who performed marvellous tangos. He became a regular and I was his regular tango partner. Unfortun- ately, in those pre-feminist days, as soon as the music changed, he would walk off the floor and leave me standing. He spoke no English but was allowed to join the ranks of the Broadway's lame ducks whom we all befriended.

Among that community was Little Trumbs. Shivering in a thin cotton dress, winter and summer, she would come in each Monday morning as I was cleaning out and refurbishing the display window and ask timidly, 'Miss, any trumbs?' Needless to say, we staff did our best to make crumbs for her.

Then there was the old chap who regularly threw faints and every time we rushed to help him we could just about read the pathetic murmur on his lips: Brandy . . .

On the other hand, some of the regulars were Tartars. 'Madam' – reputed to be a retired bank manager – used to ask for a single potato cake, not to be handled manually but to be wrapped in greaseproof paper, placed in a bag and tied with string. On one occasion, a kitchen girl disturbed him when she popped unexpectedly into the restaurant: 'Madam,' he roared at her, 'you may cancel the order for the socks.' She had promised to knit him a pair.

We were plagued by up-and-coming criminals who would snatch a box of chocolates or a packet of sweets and make a dash for it. It was my misfortune once to chase and catch one. Then I had to go through the horror of the Children's Court and had the misfortune to find myself sitting beside the young villain's poor mother, who cried her eyes out during the entire proceedings.

We hated All Ireland Football Final day, when we could not move in the crush. The standard order that day was for 'tea and meat' – with 'a bit of confectionery' for the ladies. But – a curiosity for the sociologists – on any day when Cavan played in Croke Park, we suffered the highest percentage of loss from clients leaving without paying their bills.

During my Broadway days, I ogled, with the others, Jack Doyle and Movita, thrilled to see Bob Hope in the flesh, envied the legs on the Royalettes. And when I think of the clients now, the arts and music come mostly to mind. Lord and Lady Longford from the Gate Theatre were regular patrons, as were the crowd from the Abbey Theatre just round the corner. We all loved Ria Mooney, Bríd Ni Loingsigh, May Cluskey, Harry Brogan, F. J. McCormack and his wife, Eileen Crowe, Phyllis Ryan, Máire Ni Dhómhnaill and the Golden brothers. W. B. Yeats, his wife George, and their two children, Anne and Michael, ate with us, so did Maude Gonne McBride, whom I remember as a tall, slim, elegant lady in black widow's weeds.

Lennox Robinson, on the other hand, was not popular with us. He was tall, lean and cranky, with a small Sealyham dog at the end of a long lead. We despised Patrick Kavanagh for his gruff manners. He fell for Moonbeam, one of our waitresses – so-called because her granny had been a Moonbeam, a member of the chorus line at the Queen's. She spurned Kavanagh, however, showing the poor man nothing but disdain.

Along the way we entertained Josef Locke, the Walton family (and Leo Maguire, whose catchline for the Walton-sponsored programme was 'If you feel like singing, do sing an Irish song'), the gracious Australian diva Joan Sutherland and the stalwarts of the Dublin Grand Opera Society, who rehearsed in the Music Room.

And for some reason that now escapes me, we referred to Siobhan McKenna as 'Mad Mary'.

I am still in touch with some of the survivors: one happily travelling the world with her rich American, another with her Canadian in St John, Newfoundland, a third with her rancher from Moosejaw, Saskatchewan, and a fourth who married a Danish naval officer – he went to sea two days after the wedding and never came back.

After the Broadway changed hands, it traded for decades as Cafolla's. It is now a cyber café.

The Argentinian was not the only dancing partner my

mother had; in fact, she was regularly sent to dance with all sorts of officers – under the chaperoning eye of Mrs Hudson, the Broadway's manager.

Many years later, as a young lad, the writer Peter Sheridan was sent to work as a commis chef in the kitchen of another Dublin restaurant. It will remain nameless for reasons that will be clear when you hear that one of the activities in its kitchen was flicking tea-towels at the food to remove the cockroaches. The exterminators, when finally called in, actually used shovels to remove the piles of insect corpses.

A chef was hired for this kitchen, a fascinating Italian whose nose hair, according to Sheridan, thickly decorated his upper lip like a moustache. He was also stereotypically loud and colourful, every tiny incident in his sphere of activity inflated to the level of operatic drama. So, he was temperamental and 'difficult', but fascinating to the fourteen-year-old nascent writer, dramatist and film-maker, who never forgot him.

Cut to thirty-five years later and Sheridan is now a successful playwright, author and film-maker. He also continues to be active in the community affairs of his local docklands. He is looking at photographs of a community-theatre project and talking to one of the people involved, who looks Italian.

It is the nose-moustached-one's son.

It turns out the Italian chef was one of these sailors on a ship interned at the North Wall for the duration of the war. The men were let off it for one day a week. It is quite likely that he met his Irish wife between dances with my mother in the Broadway Café.

Pubs and Dubs and Some Square Mile

There was a time in Peter Sheridan's Dublin when 'difference' was just that: handicap, mental or physical, could be tolerated so families, especially large ones, would absorb the afflicted member and get on with it. No longer. All must now strive, achieve and, if they cannot, they are labelled societal failures.

It has to be said, of course, that this was also the era when some unlucky souls, inconveniently raucous or even just socially embarrassing, could be put away in 'asylums' to be hidden from the neighbours and safely forgotten.

'Achievement', though, can be mercurial. It evolves with fashions, norms and even economies. In his introduction to *Luke Kelly, A Memoir*, by Des Geraghty, Sheridan recalls that on the walls of his school, the photographs commemorated not people like Luke but those who had been called to the priesthood – or those rarities (within his neighbourhood along the North Wall docks) who had been granted that supreme accolade: a university degree.

Sheridan did get a degree and while, as a consequence, his reputation in his birthplace rose above those of his peers, he himself did not.

His personality includes a 'quintessential Dub' strand and he plays it when necessary, giving great 'Dub' to chat-show hosts when he is on the publicity trail with his books or the plays he directs.

Despite the coruscating humour, however, he is a serious man whose view of his childhood is simultaneously rose-coloured and realistic. He does not conceal the poverty, the polio epidemics, the ugly iron callipers on small thin legs, Little Willie (the poster child for an institution in Baldoyle), the horror of children beaten to a pulp by their teachers in God's name. In conversation and in his work, he acknowledges the general climate of fear: of hell's retribution, of Communism (remember the prayer for the conversion of Russia?), of authority in general. He has also reached an honest view of himself, faults and all.

Although he can't help me with the specificity of the Seven Churches ritual, his knowledge of Dublin is deep. He is wonderful company and, in his writer's brain, compassionate and fully operational from an early age, there is a theatrical storehouse housing a panoply – 'a complete and splendid array', according to my *Concise Oxford Dictionary* – of the quirky, the uncommon and the intrinsic humanity of even the most annoying or criminally inclined of his fellow Dubliners. 'Panoply' is the most fitting word I can come up with for this fizzing population of characters, their peculiarities and the anecdotes they attract, yet it is not fully accurate because Sheridan's storehouse is still expanding.

The book he was writing when we met, another for Patricia Scanlan's *Open Door* literacy series, was triggered by an inner-city kid he didn't know but whom he had heard about: 'People tell me things.'

This kid's nickname was Snowball and his constant companion was a terrier with asymmetrical ears: one reached for the stars, the other stuck out sideways, parallel to the ground. Snowball named his little dog 'Champ'.

'Snowball loved this dog, loved Champ, mad about Champ, everything was "Champ Champ Champ".' But every other kid in the neighbourhood called the dog 'Three O'Clock'. Snowball resented this, to the extent that should he overhear this calumny, he morphed into the Hound of Heaven, chasing down the perpetrator to the ends of the earth, or at least Sheriff Street . .

Along with its denizens, chronicled so vividly in his novels and memoirs, Sheridan's mental storehouse also contains sounds and smells of the city, particularly of Seville Place, Sheriff Street and their surrounds. Of all the senses, it is said by 'experts' (of whom the world is full), smell is the strongest prompter of childhood recall. Peter Sheridan would agree. His childhood Dublin was a city of odours. 'I used to do messages for my father when I was a kid, so I got to know different places, all with different smells.'

Proximity to the Liffey was a mixed blessing when the tide was out – 'The stench was terrible sometimes', as it was when the wind blew from the direction of the knacker's yard in Ardee Street. But down by the Four Courts, 'the fruit market was unlike anything else when you walked through it of a morning'. Outside the Sheridans' house in the evening, it was the odour of drying manure left by the cattle going to the North Wall. 'A country smell in the city. Seemed like a contradiction.'

He looks off through a window into the lush back garden of the house in Whitehall he shares with his wife, Sheila, two Labradors and a rotating cast of grown-up children and other relatives. He is not seeing the roses. He is re-creating his old neighbourhood where poultry, too, left traces in the air: 'Just off Oriel Street there was a chicken farm. It was owned by the Ahearns. I knew them because Mog Ahearn was a drummer with Full Circle. And just before the chicken place, a family called Shepherds had a log farm. They chopped the logs there, so there was always the smell of wet wood.' And there was a real farm in his own family: 'My grandfather had a city farm, with cows, horses and chickens, at the back of Friary Avenue off Smithfield.'

Jim Sheridan, an Old IRA man, lived with his wife, Elizabeth, a Connollyite Volunteer, in a 'city farmhouse' that, in addition to its front door, had big double doors leading into its stableyard. 5A Friary Avenue was a laneway connecting Smithfield with the back of the Capuchin church on Church Street.

This grandfather was 'a total Sinn Féiner' who 'lost total faith in Dev when he formed Fianna Fáil, just stayed out of that whole FF thing.' It was he who gave the (very) young Peter his first drink – when he and his sister went to visit during the interval of a pantomime in the Father Mathew Hall. 'A glass of port. I can remember the stage spinning around when I went back into the hall and I couldn't understand why. I always associated my grandfather with alcohol as a result and it was only years later I discovered he was teetotal. All his life.'

Like every Dubliner who endured the winter smog before Mary Harney's ban on 'smoky coal', Sheridan's memories of the central city include the acrid stink of coal – coal smoke, coal dust and so on – but what was uncommon was the additional tang introduced by the wineries under the bridge close to his home. A series of bonded wine cellars owned by companies such as John Whites and Twohigs, they ran all the way from the bridge to Sheriff Street. Unfortunately, what they emitted was not a bouquet, but an 'alcoholicky' pong.

As he got older, the scents of Dublin meant less to Sheridan than her pubs. Cornerstone was the Liverpool bar, on the quayside where the boats docked; Sheridan Senior worked at the Shelbourne dog track and 'Every evening, my mother left the house at ten thirty and went to the Liverpool where she had his pint ready when he walked in the door, having parked his bike in the hallway.'

His mother and father drank almost every night 'but totally in moderation'. They spread their custom – for instance, to Bertie Donnellys on the corner of Guild Street. 'Donnelly was a world-famous cyclist who won a silver medal in the 1928 Olympics even though his wheel burst just before the line. (He was posthumously awarded a gold.) 'Bertie lived in Mulhuddart and he used to cycle in every day. He'd open the pub, run the pub for the day and night and then cycle home.'

There was the Ball Alley on Emerald Street, Noctors, 'which is still there, the only surviving pub in that area from the time I was a kid, and the Railway Bar on the opposite corner, which was run by a family called Smith.'

Burns's bar was just down the quays at Gill Street 'and the reason that bar meant so much to me was that it had a bookie's right next door to it called Bet With Security. My Da would go in there. Or he would send me down there to place his bets.'

Some premises were visited only on special occasions, one being the Sunset Bar – he drags out the syllables for dramatic emphasis, 'The Su-unset Baa-r . . . If my father went to the races in the Phoenix Park and he won, we would stop there on the way home to have lemonade and crisps.' And if they were really 'poshing it', there were two more hostelries on his parents' approved list. One was Gaffney's in Fairview. The reason for patronage there was that young Peter's godfather lived nearby. 'My father would put on a suit and tie to go for a drink in that pub.' Most exotic of all, however, was Lloyds in Amiens Street, the first (self-described) cocktail lounge in Dublin. 'Cocktails. For some reason that appealed to my Ma and Da.'

There was a hierarchy, 'a kind of snob value', to these peregrinations. 'They wouldn't drink in Sheriff Street because that was slightly too close to "that crowd up there in the flats". We lived in a house.' (This apartheid is somewhat inexplicable because day to day, the Sheridans mixed freely with flats people when many house people would not.)

Even as a child of ten or eleven, the young Peter never went to bed before midnight. 'They'd come home at twenty past or half eleven and my father would hold forth with the lodgers.'

In his writing, he has chronicled the paying guests his family took in, some transient, others less so. The transients included English holidaymakers: 'It just seems unimaginable now, but people would come and spend their summer holidays in our house!' From Liverpool and Manchester mostly, they 'would go out into town for the day, have a few drinks, come back, have their dinner, and then go off with my Ma and Da to the Liverpool, come back to the house, have a few more drinks, have the Row or as my da called it, "a bit of a discussion". This usually dissolved into a sing-song.'

A Lancashire man, a Mr Harris, came annually for fifteen years. He had escaped the North Strand bombing in May 1941 and, year after year, bent the Sheridan family's collective ear with stories about this bombing and his exploits in the Second World War. 'He'd keep you up until five or six in the morning if you'd let him and every year, around June or July, when we knew Mr Harris was coming there was war in our house about who'd have to share a room with him because you'd be condemned to chit-chat all night.'

Pubs, actual and as material in the re-creation of childhood memories for his work, continued into Peter Sheridan's adulthood. 'They became a big part of my world in my twenties and thirties because I was a big drinker then, and when people came to visit Dublin, specially theatre people, I would bring them on a pub tour of Dublin. Especially pubs with literary associations.'

For example, the Behans, who lived in Russell Street at the back of Croke Park, drank in Gills nearby. And Fluther Goods – named after the character in O'Casey's *The Plough and the Stars* and now Clonliffe House – was not too far away in Ballybough. This house displayed a photograph of the real Fluther Good, apparently a local carpenter.

Seán O'Casey did purloin real people's names for the characters in his plays, if not necessarily their personalities. But when he became famous, several people sued him, sometimes successfully when they could prove he had portrayed them recognisably. Sheridan himself was born on Abercorn Road where O'Casey had lived for a while, and when, as a youngster, he was delivering newspapers on behalf of the Legion of Mary, the street was on his route. 'The woman in number thirteen used say to me (*sniff, lips tight with scorn*): "I took that Seán O'Casey to court and I got thirty shillings off of him!"' She had won her case because she proved that in the *Shadow of a Gunman*, Mrs Henderson had been based on her, even though her name was Murphy.

'And funnily enough the family that lived in number eighteen were called Boyle.' This, though, was probably coincidence because the real Captain Boyle in *Juno and the Paycock* proved much closer to home. 'Years later I discovered a connection within my own family. My sister Ita is married to a man called Rafferty. His mother is a woman called Boyle, and her father was known around the area as Captain Jackie Boyle.' By the time Sheridan became interested, however, there was no one left alive to verify the connection.

When he guided his visitors around the pubs, he so-o loved shocking them with sightings of the guy who dressed in a gorilla suit. He got to know this man when he was rehearsing plays in rooms on Parnell Square. 'You'd see him in places like the Avondale House and the cafeteria up there. He'd be sitting at the bar. With the gorilla's head on the counter. A stranger would come in and he'd pop on the head, and someone would say to the stranger, "Would ya look at your man!"' And stand back.

Or what about the (serious) story of the man who blew up Lawless's pub on Ballybough Road and who offered in his defence that he was just walking by the pub? 'And the judge said to him that he must be the first guy who was ever blown *into* an explosion rather than away from it. The accused, you see, was found in the toilet. He was covered with soot.

Sheridan's visitors asked frequently for pubs with sing-songs so he brought them to the Sunset, especially on Sunday nights – 'Women took over the sing-song in the Sunset on Sunday nights.'

Among Peter Sheridan's talents is acting and he instinctively characterises any anecdote.

Peter: 'In order to be allowed sing on a Sunday night you had to go through the women. You'd have men begging, *begging*, to be allowed to sing.'

Woman In Charge: '"You sit down there, Paddy. You're not singing tonight."'

Peter: 'There was an amazing character there called Mick Ryan, finest interpreter of a song I ever heard.'

Mick: (*torso rigid, tone nasal, hands beseeching*): '"Cecilia! You're breaking my heart . . ." (*voice cracks*).'

Peter: 'He sang that song like it was a piece of opera. It was magnificent! I remember him singing it one night and in the middle of it he just walked out of the shop!'

Motley chorus (*begging*): '"Aahh, Mick, come back, come *back*! Come back and *finish* the *song*—"'

Peter: 'But off he went and wouldn't come back. Whoever Cecilia was, she made him very upset!'

He *loves* that story. Pauses to enjoy it anew.

Pubs occupy a different place in society now, not only in the area of the North Wall, but there the changes may be more stark than they are anywhere else in the country. 'If you make a square, starting in Sheriff Street, down to the quays, up to Commons Street and back around again, there were probably thirty pubs. There are probably three now.' It is not hard to figure out why. It is attributed to many things:

'regeneration' is one. 'That area – that square mile – has probably seen the greatest and most radical societal change in the whole country.'

There are other words too, such as 'modernisation': 'In 1955 there were five thousand men employed on the docks. There are probably fifty now, and with the destruction of the flats there isn't a huge proletarian population in the immediate area. Men working the river went into the pubs at lunchtime for a few pints, went back to work and then went in again for a few pints on the way home at six o'clock. That was the routine.'

No dockers, no pubs.

He is sanguine about the changes, but perhaps uneasy too. When they married, Sheila and he borrowed money and paid for their mobile home on Windmill Road in Crumlin at the rate of twelve pounds a month. 'The one and only time I lived on the southside. I've been trying to hide it ever since! We never went on a holiday, never ate out in a restaurant, but we had a great time and we never worried.

'Then we moved to Ballybough and then we moved to this nice house here and we have an apartment in Spain – and we're worried?' His expression is disbelieving yet speaks volumes. Interest rates. Bubbles bursting. All that.

'You really do have to work very hard to keep things in perspective, but I'm reflective of hundreds of thousands of people out there. For Irish people, this is the first time it's been like this. All through the centuries we had the sense that history had screwed us and we held on to that, but here we are at the beginning of the twenty-first century and we find that we're at the heart of Europe and there's money, and the population is increasing and we have rights and entitlements . . .'

It's dizzying. 'One of the things I never understood when I was young was how rich people could be mean. Sure when you'd loads of money what was the point of being mean?' But he regularly hears conversations of people 'who congregate to talk about how to hold on to their wealth' and he sort of understands. A bit.

Asked what he would miss about Dublin if he was forced out of it, the answer is instant, 'The talk. I'm someone who engages with people when I'm out. I engage with the world and I find that people tell me things about themselves. Stories. It passes the time, as Sam Beckett might have said, but that's not it. I think that as a people we just have a natural curiosity in a way that other nationalities don't have.

'When we go to America we are naturally asking questions, how the society works, how the people fit in. I would miss that hugely. Even when I go over to Spain and I'm mixing with English and Scots, Germans and Spanish, after about a week I begin to notice that there's a lack of engagement among the people I meet. They seem much more satisfied with their lot.

'There is a natural curiosity in Dublin. I can talk with people in shops, on buses. People don't shrink and they do tell you the most fascinating stories and reveal the most fascinating things. I don't have any barriers. My father was like that too.'

His love of and immersion in theatre came from his father, who won a couple of actors' awards. He played Captain Boyle in *Juno*, Seumus Shields in *Gunman* on the amateur circuit, then quit. 'By his late forties he had done what he needed to do. He had given Jim [Sheridan's film-maker brother] and me a start and he knew, just knew, that we were going to take up the ball.'

Peter Sheridan's credentials as an 'Essential Dubliner' are impeccable, so he is the ideal person to give his view on what constitutes such a character. For the purposes of this book, this has to refer to the past; clichéd heart-of-the-rowl Dubliners are a rare breed in this era when most of the trading on Moore Street, the stereotypical Dublin thoroughfare, is carried on by people who are of African, Asian, East European or of Baltic origin.

'Openness and friendliness,' he says.

Himself, obviously.

'But a sort of perversity as well.'

Himself again.

'The Dub is always attempting to prove something to the world. We feel we've been made lesser because of the association with the bigger city, London, across the water. Maybe that's not just a Dublin thing but an Irish thing too. That feeling of having lost the language and all the kind of historical stuff that must be buried somewhere in the communal psyche. We use English but with a Gaelic consciousness.'

He gives an example. 'You have a definite "yes" and "no" in English but you don't in Gaelic, where it's "sea" and "ní hea". They translate as "Well, maybe it is and maybe it isn't." So you're saying "maybe" to everything. And then there's that whole thing where you're paying someone a compliment by using the opposite. "Ya effing bastard!" means "you're a great guy" – but to call someone "a great guy" means you're a bit iffy about him.'

There's a First City sense of 'up yours' too, softened with subtle humour.

'Dublin rose up in 1916 and Cork was asleep. And then Cork woke up and made up for it by going mad republican for the next ten years. But Dublin had done it. We let other people finish the job. That's the Dub sense of humour: you won't get one up on me, son. You might try but it won't work.'

Or: 'They're replacing flagstones outside the Gresham Hotel. You know how it is, a pile of cement, a couple of planks going over the mess so that people can still use the hotel, a couple of barrels to warn them. Ten guys there, nine leaning on shovels and one guy actually working, cutting and shearing and shrieking away with ancient cutting equipment. There's an engineering conference and the delegates are going in and they're looking at this and they can't believe it. The Spanish delegation goes in. The French delegation goes in. The German delegation is going in and one guy just can't hold himself back: "Who's in charge of the site?"

'"That fella down there—"

'So he goes down. "Are you in charge of this site?"

'"Yes, I am. I'm the gaffer."

'"You know, in Germany now when we cut the pavement we have a computer on the site. And everything is punched into the computer and we are correct to one ten-thousandth of a centimetre."

'And the Dublin guy says, "Well, that wouldn't do us at all. Because we have to be spot on!"'

O'Sullivan's Valet

The Gresham, scene of many interviews for this book, is very swish these days with, at the time of writing, not a stonecutter in sight.

There are still faces in the lobby and the posh new bar that I recognise from many years ago, but Paddy Hanlon's isn't one of them. Paddy has retired. He is eighty-six now, a gently mannered man with a soft voice and big, work-roughened hands. He is too modest, shy even, to talk directly to me but one of his daughters, Patricia, fills in for him.

If Bests' Savile Row cutter of independent means lived *in* the hotel, Paddy (who would have known him and may even have carried his bags) and his family lived *off* it. And not only because of the wages.

Paddy was fourteen years of age when he joined the Gresham staff as a bellboy and general factotum. He was an institution there for more than four decades, during which, among his other duties, he washed the plate glass on the hotel porch and polished the brass at its regal entrance. He got up at four o'clock in the morning to cycle from his Marino home to wake the Americans who had to catch ships or planes. He met guests when they arrived at the North Wall docks, or at Busarus, hefting their suitcases all the way back to the hotel. Occasionally his job entailed meeting country people under Clerys clock, the only Dublin land- mark some of them knew.

And one Saturday he was vacuuming the main staircase when there was a tremendous explosion. The bomb wrecked five first-floor bedrooms, and the waterfall that immediately followed ruined the stairs and sent a number of staff scurrying home, never to return. Not Paddy. Family was his priority but the Gresham was his life.

His boss, Toddy O'Sullivan, ran the hotel like a firm, fair, but benevolent father, generous with his staff while insisting on high standards. 'Women with ten, maybe fifteen kids to look after,' says his daughter, 'worked in the Gresham and fed their kids out of it. Waitresses married chefs, had kids, and then the kids were taken into the Gresham family. And it was a family. People cut each other's hair.'

Ever present on the floor of his domain, Toddy noticed everything, even minor sartorial slippages such as a crooked or sloppily knotted tie. Spotting one such, he would call over its owner, retie it and then, with a little pat, 'Off you go now.'

When Paddy married Margaret, a girl from Kerry who worked in the Clarence, it was his boss who signed all the necessary documents guaranteeing a mortgage for the house in Marino. As well he might. For Paddy worked not only in the hotel. His duties included escorting the O'Sullivan children to school and collecting them afterwards, shopping for Mrs O'Sullivan, sometimes cooking and cleaning for her, even helping her choose her clothes. And when Toddy was invited to a function, Paddy went ahead of him with the outfit and, acting almost as valet, helped him into it.

His family life was frugal. Sheets from the Gresham that were past their sell-by dates went home on the back of Paddy's bike, were darned and bleached by his wife, then had a long, useful life on the family beds.

This nothing-goes-to-waste ethos extended to the Boss, who, every time the Gresham was refurbished or the décor changed, encouraged his employees to bring home whatever was now *de trop*, carpets, curtains, even furniture and fittings: 'We were the only house in Marino with a chandelier!' Patricia also remem- bers the family's lovely blue car- pet, whose only flaw was its liberal embellishment with the letter 'G'. 'We explained that away to visitors by telling them Mammy's name was Geraldine.' As for the gorgeous wing arm- chair, placed proudly in the front window, 'We covered up that 'G' with an antimacassar from Guineys.'

Dress and dinner dances provided a bonanza. Champagne glasses that could no longer pass the 'no-chips' test came home for the family china cabinet; vol-au-vents or meringues went into the next day's school lunchboxes – 'or stuff that we thought was poison'. Pâté.

Staff and their offspring were familiar with the attractions of Mosney Holiday Camp because its owner, Billy Butlin, a hotel regular, was generous with free tickets. Particularly covetable were the American clothes deliberately left behind by those who had purchased too many Aran sweaters and whose suitcases were stuffed. Patricia remembers a beautiful dress her mother wore for years.

None of this, by the way, was seen as taking charity or other people's leftovers. Nor was it a source of embarrassment. In those days, you didn't slink into pawn shops, or conceal that something was second-hand, or pretend that Guineys and Frawleys, rather than Arnotts and Switzers, were your retailers of choice.

For instance, when the Gresham staff got wind of a fire sale in Guineys of North Earl Street, Paddy Hanlon rushed home on his bike during his break to inform Margaret so she could be among the crowds in North Earl Street waiting to catch the stock that Michael Guiney, it had been rumoured, was to throw from the shop's upper windows. This was the way Dublin worked at that level. People took pride in 'managing'.

It was not remarkable then that his wife supplemented Paddy's wages by taking in washing or that she regularly hocked her wedding ring when Paddy's uniform needed to be dry-cleaned. Or that she spent hour after painstaking hour embroidering intricate Celtic designs on an Irish dancing costume for a few shillings.

She used her skill at sewing to good effect in her own household, where no blouse or jumper was beyond repair. If it could not be darned or 'invisibly mended', a tear or burn hole could be disguised with an embroidered patch. Patricia, however, got short shrift when she went to work in Switzers and, obviously infected by the rarified Grafton Street air, asked her mother to embroider a patch bearing the initials 'CC' as a decorative addition to one of her outfits.

Coco Chanel, indeed! Who did that girl think she was?

Paddy Hanlon's early days also covered the era when clergy were never to be seen eating in public or attending the theatre. (When we actors made entrances or exits onto or off the Abbey stage, we had to avoid tripping over them as they stood in the wings.) In Paddy's world, a firm knock on the delivery door in Thomas Lane at the back of the hotel would herald the entrance of a three-nun posse in search of their regular treat of tea and buns in a corner of the hotel kitchen. Now and then he even brought them upstairs to an empty guest room where he served them their dinner.

A large number of famous people went through Paddy's capable hands, but secrets learned in the Gresham stayed there. It proves hard to winkle out even a few names of the 'nice' and 'lovely', impossible to discover those of the condescending and imperious.

His daughter did reveal that while he met President Kennedy with the rest of the hotel's staff during That Visit in 1963, 'it was my dad who was chosen to go around with him and get his messages. It was only for a short time. It was kept very private.'

Although they're not saying, the thirty-fifth President of the United States probably features in the 'nice/lovely' column, alongside Princess Grace and her husband, Prince Rainier, the pianist Russ Conway and George Best, who briefly dated one of Patricia's sisters.

No give at all, though, on who lives in the nasty column. Paddy's and his daughter's lips are zipped. But under pain of *death* if I ever reveal it, I was told the name of one Very Famous Comedian (British, still working, very funny) whose imperious and condescending manner turned everybody off. That information will go with me to my grave.

When he retired, Paddy Hanlon was given a gold watch and a key to admit him to any room in any hotel in the Gresham group, with a standing invitation to stay for any length of time. He has never taken it up.

The Reel Deal

Dubliners were, and remain, avidly interested in going to the pictures. I was introduced to movies at the State Cinema in Phibsboro, to which my mother and aunt took me to see *The Robe*. From memory, obviously unreliable, I was about four, but I have just discovered that this film was first released in 1953 so I had to have been eight.

For days beforehand they prepared me by describing what 'the pictures' was. A huge white sheet. And there were people on it. All dressed in colour. And they were moving and talking and you could follow the story through what they said, like you did with the *Sunday Play* on the radio. But this play would be about Jesus. And I could eat ice-cream in my own little tub while we were watching it.

Remember that, except for the very privileged and rich minority who could catch a snowy BBC through an 'aerial', this was pre-television in Ireland. To me, pictures, coloured or not, were in books.

Within minutes of the film's start I was hooked – but knocked for six by the decibels booming in my ears and the vividness of the colour. Red wasn't red, it was blood-red, carmine. Blue wasn't blue, it was cobalt or azure. Already a bookworm, I fancied myself a connoisseur of words. And here were those words come to life.

As for the story, it was truly shocking. It was one thing to go to Mass and listen to sermons about the Crucifixion, it was another to see it in technicolour, magnified a dozen times. And when Jesus's seamless robe took on a life of its own to wrap itself round the neck of the vile Roman soldier at the foot of the cross, strangling him, I almost fainted with terror. I had nightmares for weeks and months afterwards.

Nevertheless, I was definitely and uncritically snared. Who cared if Victor Mature, as Demetrius, spoke as though he was simultaneously gargling California wine or that Richard Burton's ancient Roman accent came direct from RADA? I certainly didn't and from then on, good, bad or mediocre, films meant enchantment and I regularly squandered two-thirds of my sixpence-a-week pocket money on the fourpenny rush at the 'Boh'.

At such a price, the young Saturday clientele at the Bohemian Cinema in Phibsboro was varied and hard to control – so much so that kids were regularly flung out by the hard-pressed ushers. I was always prissily glad to see the messers go. We were trying to *watch the film*, for God's sake – even if the Boh thought kids were interested only in stupid western foller-uppers and cartoons. A film was a film was a film.

At one time there were eight cinemas on or near O'Connell Street. Some, like the Savoy, the Ambassador and the Royal, were not strictly cinemas but converted theatres or concert halls. Some did not object when their patrons danced in the aisles. I remember being quietly proud when my own parents confessed that they had sprung to their feet to rock and roll between the seats during a showing of *Rock Around the Clock* in the Carlton. Some combined film with variety shows. The Savoy auditorium seated more than two thousand, while the Theatre Royal held double that number and offered the full theatre experience.

We sure got value for our admission ticket at the Royal, with a Marx Brothers, Laurel and Hardy or a Charlie Chaplin film, a variety show, which frequently included a complete one-act play, comedy sketches, Jimmy Campbell's live orchestra, an Audience Participation Quiz with a prize of half-a-crown and, in the interval, many people's favourite, Tommy Dando. The house-lights came on and the curtains swished open to show a blank white screen and then, to the thunderous strains of 'Keep Your Sunny Side Up! (Up!)', Tommy, chubby on the little seat attached to the massive theatre organ, rose smoothly from the orchestra pit into a rainbow of light. He rode that organ as though it were an unruly yearling, pounding and pedalling to get the last ounce of power out of it.

After 'Sunny Side' we clapped, cheered, then cleared our throats because we knew what was coming. And there it was, up on the screen: the words of the next song. A flourish from Tommy and all we had to do was to follow the bouncing ball as it hopped shakily from word to word.

Sometimes it fell behind us, sometimes it ran ahead or even disappeared, but it didn't matter. We knew where we were going. We gave ourselves huge rounds of applause. We risked damage to the carpet with our stamping invitation to 'come into the parlour' because we were Irish and there was a welcome for us on the mat. We swayed in our seats and even held hands with the perfect stranger in the next seat as we begged 'Daisy, Daisy' to give us her answer do. We followed Dorothy 'Somewhere Over the Rainbow', yearned for 'Red Sails in the Sunset', admired 'Galway Bay' and, of course, because we were Dubliners, screeched lustily about cockles and mussels alive, alive-oh.

I even remember – or maybe this is my tendency to dramatise – that on one occasion we all stood respectfully to bellow a full-hearted 'Faith of Our Fathers'. I do know for sure that at the end of every joint performance, when Tommy struck up 'Sunny Side' again and began slowly to sink back into the pit, I always felt replete – as though I had enjoyed a really good dinner.

Some cinemas also boasted ballrooms; a dress dance at the Metropole was a very swanky affair. Its spot prizes were not your packet of Sweet Afton or your pair of braces, but a large box of Dairy Milk or even a ten-shilling note. Many incorporated tearooms or full restaurants; the Savoy gave equal billing to its cinema and restaurant on its canopy. From O'Connell Street, you could follow the direction indicated by a classy illuminated sign, white letters on a black background, to the Capitol Cinema on Princes Street. Its beautiful staircase had been fashioned for the SS *Titanic* but had not fitted properly.

For me, 'treat' afternoons there included not only the film, *High Society*, for instance, but a spell in the tearoom with its flocked wallpaper and tables lit with small red lamps. This was a place where silver cutlery, teapots and condiment sets were heavy and where fancies were delivered on tiered cake stands by waitresses who wore caps and white gloves. I remember them as middle-aged, maternal and always smiling – but I was young at the time. They might have been in their twenties or thirties.

The Metropole closed in 1968, the Capitol in 1972. The Plaza Cinerama round the corner from Coláiste Mhuire on Parnell Square, originally an eighteenth-century chapel, morphed into the Wax Museum. The Carlton is derelict and, at the time of writing, is locked in legal dispute. On Eden Quay, no trace remains of the Corinthian or the Astor, where I first saw 'foreign' films and fell in love with Sisi, the Empress of Austria. The Adelphi, which regularly rested its projectors to host live shows from big stars, such as Cliff Richard and the Rolling Stones, is now part of Arnotts. The Grafton, which specialised in cartoons, will be God-knows-what in a continually changing Grafton Street. Where is the Cameo, which was on Middle Abbey Street, or the Regent, in Cathal Brugha Street? Or the Pillar Picture House under Nelson's stony gaze?

Now there are far more screens in the city than ever there were. It is all very efficient, computerised and clean, with almost as much emphasis on the gargantuan amounts of food and drink you are encouraged to bring to your seat as there is on the film. I acknowledge progress: the revamped Savoy is terrific and the UCG is clean comfortable and, what's more, offers car parking.

But I do miss those rainy afternoons in the sixties when, as a young Abbey actress with time to kill between morning rehearsals and an evening show, I would sit virtually alone in the Savoy's worn seats, inhaling the stink of old cigarette smoke while waiting for my exclusive showing.

I saw *West Side Story* five times there. And each time, as the lights went down and the curtains peeled away to reveal the pristine blankness of the screen, I reached into my handbag for my new tube of Rowntree's fruit gums, prised out a green one and settled into that place where there is no drizzle to ruin hair or good coats, and where the problems are somebody else's.

An Aristotelian Polity

Until recently, RTÉ, and Radio Éireann before it, employed many variety artists when 'Light Entertainment' was an important subset of the broadcaster's remit. The station could still be seen as an accommodating microsystem, comprising wildly brilliant people of widely differing talents.

Some were and are voluble and eccentric, such as film-maker Bob Quinn and television-producer-turned-pundit Senator Eoghan Harris. Others, like musicians Peter Brown and Paddy Glacken, are so quiet that they come into view only when their work surfaces in the wider public.

Many find refuge at the station for a time, are enabled to further their talents alongside their jobs, then leave to launch themselves on the world. Two exquisite writers, John McKenna and Aidan Mathews, have stayed.

I have seized the opportunity to talk to the latter about himself and his city but also, I had heard, he was just the man to help in the hunt for the elusive identification of my Seven Churches. 'Ah, yes, the Seven Churches. You got a Plenary Indulgence for that, you know, in the good old days of supernatural numeracy.'

Mathews, whose day job is as a producer of radio drama and religious programmes, is by vocation a writer of fiction, plays, poetry and dissertations on life, love and the works of God. He comes from Donnybrook, and is keenly aware of the privilege of his birth into the large, prosperous family of a successful surgeon, with a godfather who was Chief Justice and later President.

Although the Donnybrook of his childhood was predominantly middle class, it was not universally so: 'You might have had families with ten or twelve children in each of the Pembroke cottages, now typically occupied perhaps by a single individual with a cat.'

His sense of humour is apposite and penetrating, yet so subtle that the penny drops sometimes a couple of beats after he has let it go. He is gentle of voice, courteous to a fault; to talk to him, even with the concentration necessary to take in the uncommon profundity of what he says and his extraordinary vocabulary, is to relax, even with the hiss of coffee machines and the high octane buzz of intellectual chat (not!) in the coffee dock of the Radio Centre.

He is a deeply committed, but not myopic, Roman Catholic and regular churchgoer. 'When I was a kid we'd walk to the village to get the messages. And whether it was groceries or a newspaper, you'd always drop into the church en route to light a candle and say a prayer. It was in no way unusual or remarkable.'

He mourns the current fall-off in churchgoing among the wider, now hugely dispersed city community. Worse, 'A huge number of the citizens of this city – now extending from Drogheda to Arklow and in as far as Mullingar – live in new municipal areas which are not beautiful. That is a sin against the Holy Spirit.' But in this fall-off, he has observed something unexpected. 'After the Papal Mass in 1979 which was the funeral games for Catholic culture here, I expected that the bourgeois parishes would empty much more rapidly than the working-class parishes because, traditionally and typically, the Church has always been defended by the poor.'

His own parish church, the Church of the Sacred Heart, 'was built on the pennies of the poor, the traders and the domestic servants in Protestant households'. (The Spanish-born wife of Napoleon III, the Empress Eugenie, gave twenty thousand pounds, however!) 'Donnybrook Fair was a place of such violence, riot and lasciviousness that the authorities finally scotched it and, in the 1860s, the diocese undertook to build the Sacred Heart by way of atonement.

'When I was a kid, the middle class would worship discreetly in the transepts, all white mantillas and black overcoats. And the multitudinous poor would pray in the nave. Not the case now. The opposite, in fact. A genteel minority persists in its prostrations.' While in the newer parishes, in this extended Dublin, attendances may be down to five per cent and at daily Mass the age profile is elderly, 'you go to services in the prosperous parishes and the Church there still presents as comparatively robust'.

The Roman Catholic Church and Gaelscoileanna. Twin peaks of Dublin's new wealthy.

Mathews's wider Dublin in childhood and youth was 'an Aristotelian polity'. 'The word' (I looked it up) is from the Greek '*polis*', meaning city. According to the *Concise Oxford Dictionary*, it is an 'organised society; state as a political entity'. In Aristotle's time, cities were independently governed, with high walls round many of the richer ones as a defence from attacks by other cities, and therefore limited in size. Mathews explains: 'Aristotle – indeed the Greeks in general – took the view that a city state should be a certain size and no larger; that we were almost neurologically prepared to entertain covenants and contracts with a certain number of persons, and that we couldn't go beyond that. Dublin in my day maintained that measure, at least middle-class Dublin did, offering forms of camaraderie, like-mindedness and communal expectation which I mostly found comforting and familiar.'

His Dublin polity is the area between the canals on both sides of the river. It is Georgian Dublin in particular, 'a district you can't traverse without meeting someone you know', which he found 'warm and intimate and benign'.

On the evening before we met, he had had a glad experience of the city's wider communality. He was driving at about nine o'clock when he witnessed a man collapsing on the street, injuring his face, nose and mouth. 'I was the second person to reach him and within moments, seven or eight people were around, one of whom had a mobile phone, and an ambulance was called. Everyone remained with him, making him comfortable and speaking to him for the sixteen minutes it took the ambulance to arrive.'

As the ambulance left, the group said goodbye ('expressing good wishes on parting', says my trusty *Concise Oxford*), cheered by the sense of having done good and, in particular, having been part of a tiny communal endeavour. 'I was exhilarated by it, by the sense of subtle community that can animate passers-by.'

As a writer, Mathews's observational eye, 'McGahern's account of the religious bric-à-brac in someone's home', is less quotidian than that of his late colleague. 'I remember thinking that even being aware of cultic objects in that way had to mean a dispassion and detachment on his part. I wouldn't have noticed. Any more than I would have noticed a mantelpiece or the border of a carpet.

'I would have been more aware of the unusual and the extraordinary. What didn't fit. And it was only when in my student years I lost that sense of the habitual that I became desirous of possessing it. In the very moment of extinction, I snatched at it. Everything I do, I do belatedly. My only insight is hindsight.'

He has made no secret of the hound that accompanies him everywhere, always with jaws open and teeth bared, poised to bite: his black dog, his bipolar disorder. It began to take hold as 'a hairline crack' in his mind when he was at university in America. He came home to Dublin because if he was destined to be ill, he wanted to be in familiar surroundings.

He has spent parts of his life in the 'slow and dozy cosmos' of a psychiatric hospital. 'Mental illness is terrifying when you are brought up to honour the mind and the intellect as the paramount values. *Cogito ergo sum* – "I think therefore I am" – is the motto of the Western male. Intellect makes you a competent raptor in an eat-or-be-eaten world.'

He has written about this movingly: *In the Poorer Quarters* is a collection of profoundly spiritual programme scripts, based on scripture but widened to include his own life and worldview, sometimes humorous, sometimes scathing. It was broadcast on RTÉ Radio from December 2005 to December 2006, and published as a book in 2007.

With his permission, I want to quote a passage. His wife Trish who, to his eternal surprise and gratitude, has stood by him throughout, is visiting him in hospital with their tiny daughter. '. . . *a timid female infant who made strange with me on her weekend visits and who far preferred the chaplain's budgie with its pretty pastel colours and its crackly cackle to the speechless, strongly smelling man in the nightshirt who could not lift his eyes from his hands, who could not lift his hands from his lap, who could not persuade anyone in the whole hospital that his life should be ended by execution because he disgusted the Creation and should be defecated from the domain of being. In fact, he was not a human being at all. He was only a human body.*'

An image from his stay in that hospital of St John of God is so deeply lodged in my own brain that I cannot cast it off. I want to cast it off because it is in Aidan Mathews's private ownership and I have no right to it. But no matter how hard I try, I re-imagine it every day.

His telling of it is matter-of-fact. It concerns his conviction that he was so unworthy, causing so much desolation all around, that his wife would inevitably leave him. 'I would spend much of the day and the night, too, looking for the necessary small change from other dazed and preoccupied patients in the closed ward to call her and plead with her for another hundred and eighty seconds.' Surrounded though we are by cappuccino and latte-drinkers, people lounging over their *Irish Times*, *Guardian* or *Independent* newspapers, I am undone by that film of panicked scrabbling, begging, and rushing towards the public phone. I have been undone by it ever since.

And yet he had felt 'a kind of a relief' when he was committed to hospital: 'All of the conformative posturing was now over and I didn't have to simulate normality any more. The Thatcherite care-in-the-community ethos is deeply hostile because when you are in that place of melt-down and metamorphosis you want to be among persons who are recognisably in the same situation – you can discern a sort of confederacy of the injured and the self-harming. With no secular responsibility to anyone else, it was open to me to sit in a corridor for hours on end staring at my lap with no one regarding this as prohibited behaviour.'

With the help of the drug Lithium, eventual ECT and immeasurable kindness, he recovered to resume normal life and, while remaining vigilant, maintains it with regular hospital check-ups. He is not complacent about cures, however. 'My brain seems to have a mind of its own in the sense that I'm fine for a year or two and then, *ex nihilo*, I become a completely different person. It's not so much an imperceptible process over weeks and months. At a certain moment, my experience of myself and my whole being, my somatic sense of myself as an embodied person, alters, and I experience terror of the world.

'As a teenager, I used to imagine that, if you were depressed, you'd be limp and lacklustre and utterly apathetic. You'd have to be turned in the bed for fear of bedsores like an afflicted geriatric. But when I do become clinically or psychotically depressed I experience it – and it experiences me – as terror of this world and the demonic human species within it. The most dreadful delusions of persecution take possession of me. My mind and my memory falter and fail utterly, and I imagine I'm guilty of tremendous transgressions and that I'm about to be exposed and annihilated.'

It was when he came out of St John of God's after an illness of more than two years' duration that the city began to change for him. Its intimacy now provoked a sense of claustrophobia and he no longer enjoyed the prospect of meeting someone he knew every time he walked into town. 'Privacy is the privilege of a vaster metropolitan area. You don't get away with a great deal in a little polity.'

He accepts that part of the new reality of Dublin is its culture, much-reported and discussed, of violence. An increasingly random and purposeless violence, it seems: 'I can't quite account for it except that the whole tenor of the culture is quite violent now. Violence is at the homicidal heart of our entertainment industry. It seems to be as fundamental a utility as bread and shelter.'

Although the phenomenon seems to have escalated in recent years, it does not shock him: 'By the time I was ten there had been a murder and manslaughter to the left and right of me. I had the strong sense even as a child that I had been born into the heartless heart of a very violent enterprise. I think we all knew, even as little ones, that our culture was punitive and prosecutorial.'

Before meeting him, I had asked someone else instantly and instinctively to encapsulate in one word what Dublin means these days and the answer, 'frenzy', is understandable to Aidan Mathews. 'But I think that feeling of frenzy has as much to do with mood and inner weather.'

Yet if you were to believe the tabloid headlines, Dublin society is imploding and from now on, we hapless citizens must navigate our way through widespread mayhem ('violent or damaging action', 'the crime of maiming a person so as to render him or her partly or wholly defenceless'.)

The current escalation of seemingly arbitrary violence is more than mere criminality, however. It is deeper: a peeling away of superficial politesse, witnessed some years ago by Mathews – like all writers, forever on duty – in Stillorgan shopping centre. 'I watched a woman who had mislaid her child and in a nanosecond she reverted from being a reputable bourgeoise at the helm of a gleaming trolley to become something primal and Neolithic. All the intervening layers of culture and sophistication were stripped away as she became what she really was, a shrieking solitary mammalian mother missing her infant. We're all only moments away from crisis, atrocity, displacement and ruination.'

His polity, past or present, is not homogeneous. He has a 'strong sense' of the south inner city, which he sees 'is rather self-regarding and self-conscious, rather heartlessly debonair. I loved it as a student when I would go to town each morning and work in the National Library in the days when the College of Art was also in Kildare Street, and there was a Boho varsity atmosphere around that part of town, all pint glass and ponytail and paperback editions of impenetrable French philosophers.

'And then you'd cross into O'Connell Street, leading into buggyland and the fecund teeming masses.'

Warned you about the humour – in another mouth it might be insulting, but from Mathews it is insightful and affectionate. 'There is a sudden sense of life and the moist terracing of the three generations. You're conscious of children again. And of the elderly. Being part of ages and stages . . .'

Any Dublin heroes?

'I think of my godfather.' Among other things, he thanks Cearbhall Ó Dálaigh for igniting his love of the city. 'He used to walk me through it and tell me about the genealogy of every junction.' As a result he can appreciate 'the horizontal autumn light that falls across the city in the ember months',

September to December. It was probably this early aesthetic guidance that continues to nourish the joy he always feels when homing into Dublin from a trip abroad – 'the city as placenta'.

And he is fascinated by the relationship his 'most beloved' brother now has with their joint birthplace. His brother has lived in Australia since 1989 and is rearing a family there, having spent the best part of ten years serving the people of north inner Dublin in 'areas that were once quite grubby but have been gentrified greatly by the Celtic credit card. He cannot grasp the enormity of the changes and when he comes back he doesn't quite coincide with himself.

'He's not an exile or an emigrant, but an expat. Things rigidify when you go away. When he went to Australia he became quite an impassioned nationalist and a diligent Roman Catholic Christian. That's the law of some inverse ratio of presence to distance. Things like that happen the further you go from the centre towards the periphery.

'Now he has a virtual relationship with the country. He can keep in touch by satellite and so forth, but it's a hello to a hologram, in a sense. And so he's had a tantalising relationship with phantasmal images. When he comes home, when he gets off the plane, like Oisín dismounting from his horse, he ages. And I disguise his fall as a kissing of the ground.'

Mathews gets a great kick out of the 'new Irish' in his city. He was in a petrol station in Ranelagh some weeks ago 'and I said, "Shay shay," to the Chinese man at the till. It's the only Mandarin I know. It means "thank you very much". The man was taken aback, but recovered quickly and said to me, in a strong Dublin accent, "Fair play to ya!"'

He was having his hair cut 'by a man whom I took to be from either India or Pakistan. And I asked him, "Where are you from?" and he said, "Oh, I'm from Ballaghadereen!"'

And to complete this trilogy, two of his friends were standing at the bus stop in front of the Huguenot cemetery on Merrion Row. Both Gaelgeóirí, they were conversing in Irish. An elderly man passed by and, after casting them a poisonous glance, muttered into his chin, loudly enough for them to hear: '"I wish the lot of youse would fuck off back to yizzer own countries."'

As the saying goes, 'If you want to know me, walk in my shoes.' And despite my own impression of kindness and compassion, who knows what it is to compete with a black dog for possession of a man? His wife does. But 'Trish is very south-facing, a very gentle, grounded individual.' Their backgrounds could not be more dissimilar: she was born in the West of Ireland in a thatched cottage with no water or electricity, he was born 'into a large prosperous Dublin family and my birth was announced in the *Irish Times*'. He remains astonished at her constancy. He cannot believe his luck. 'The body of the beloved one becomes an ecosystem where you live and move and have your being.'

They have two daughters, twenty-one and sixteen, 'and when I tell them about my childhood in the 1960s, they regard it as very ethnic and exotic. Laura and Lucy attend the Eucharist as I do and Laura reads from the lectern as I do, but my preconciliar stories are as strange to them as Scheherezade's.

'Very bright and creative people, which is almost everybody, thank God, tend to be connected and commonsensical. Mental illness, on the other hand, is an autistic state. Contrary to the myth of redemptive insanity, it locks you in. In the long aftermath, you look in your diary and there's nothing in it except full moons and half-moons and quarter-moons because nothing has happened in the state of sterility. You hear about events like Hungerford, Lockerbie or Chernobyl and they mean nothing to you. All that happened was that you walked the corridors until there were spy-holes in your slippers.'

But he has come to an accommodation with his illness. 'It's a wonderful world, it really is. I've seen many grimly ill people become the pilgrims of their own immobility. I've seen them achieve astounding things, be transfigured rather than disfigured by their difficulties, inherit a little humility through the task of compassion, and survive to live, to become ordinary, to take on human nature itself as a form of holy orders.' There are, according to some statistics, 400,000 people in Ireland (that probably means 200,000 in Greater Dublin), the mechanics of whose minds are poised on just a sliver of a quivering globe.

In the case of Aidan Mathews, *cogito ergo sum* is another illusion. The mind is *not* the whole man here, and I hope that some day you, too, may have the privilege of conversing with him, Dubliner to Dubliner, so enjoyably that you will even forget to pursue your quarry – the identification of those Seven Churches . . .

Wouldn't Suit the Sugar Boiling

When one hears the words 'Donnybrook' and 'lasciviousness' in the same context from Aidan Mathews, one thinks not of Larry Gogan, the Peter Pan of Irish broadcasting. But it turns out that Larry has a secret.

Many years ago, he and his beloved Florrie went dancing at the Crystal Ballroom, famous all over Dublin for its prismatic mirrored glass ball. Towards the end of each evening, usually during a slow set, the regular house-lights were dimmed and this ball was spotlit and set to revolve, conferring beauty on the plain, mystique on the ordinary. This magic moment always elicited a communal 'Oooh' even amongst the regulars.

So here they are, Larry and Florrie, shimmering with rainbows and drifting contentedly along the sprung dance-floor in the midst of the crowd. Next thing, he gets a tap on the shoulder. He looks round. It's management, on patrol. With a jerk of a thumb over its shoulder, it emits a growled: 'Off!'

'We were thrown off the floor for lurching!'

'Lurching' was the term employed by Dubliners to

describe what non-Dubliners might refer to as 'close dancing' – 'wearing', for those of us from Ballymun.

Sinless Larry Gogan? Lurching?

'Yeah, it's true. We were. Asked to leave the floor. By the management.'

After year upon cheery year of broadcasting pop, he talks in short, staccato sentences.. Like his boyhood hero, Alan Freeman. 'The power in that man's voice. The way he used it. And no waffle. Straight to the point.'

Beneath the Radio Centre's coffee shop is the studio underworld, to which, as in prisons, entry is effected by electronic tags, disembodied voices on speakers and visual identification. Its carpeted corridors and sound- proofed walls absorb footsteps and speech so that humans seem strangely disembodied. Lined with heavy doors above which red or green lights glow to signify that studios are live or on standby, this four-sided sanctum is hollowed out round a central courtyard, designed as a resource for light and fresh air, but on this July day of a monsoon summer, it reflects only the dripping grey sky above it.

It is lunchtime, and in prospecting for somewhere quiet to talk, we find that the vast Studio One is empty. This is where orchestras rehearse and sometimes give concerts, and where celebratory or valedictory parties are held. We feel a little like trespassing children as we settle beside the conductor's podium and I switch on my tape-recorder to listen to one of the most instantly recognisable and distinctive voices not only in Dublin, but in the country.

Contrary to what most of his fans believe – that he is a northsider – Larry Gogan was born in Rathgar. In his grandfather's time, the Gogans owned a chain of sixteen shops in the city and Larry was taken into the business. In some circles, his grandfather was reputed to have invented the after-dinner mint.

The Gogans certainly made their own sweets and Larry remembers watching the sugar-boilers working in the factory at the back of the family's premises in Fairview: the heat under the huge cauldrons on which the sugar was boiled down, the long steel counter on which, when liquefied, it was poured in shining sheets. He was mesmerised by the way the men handled it, at how, while it was still warm, they lifted it in long, sloopy strings and slung it up on to overhead hooks, then pulled, manipulated and stretched it until it was thin enough to be shaped and chopped into fruit drops, acid drops, 'all sorts of hard sweets. They weren't wrapped in those days.'

Mesmerised or not, though, from an early age Larry, one of Radio Luxembourg's most avid fans, knew where his destiny lay. As it happened, a woman named Maura Fox, who worked for Janus, a PR company, was a regular customer at one of the shops. Young Gogan discovered that she was 'in the know' with Radio Éireann and asked her brazenly to get him an audition. He was on his way into broadcasting, via 'a couple of little acting jobs'.

Cut to many, many years later and in front of six hundred guests, including the crowned royalty in every strand of Irish music, U2, Corrs, Chieftains, Westlife *et al*, he is receiving yet another of the myriad awards he has garnered in his forty-five-year broadcasting career. This from Bob Geldof: 'We had few champions in this country – there are benchmark people in every country's broadcasting. In Ireland there's Gay and there's Larry. These men had a profound effect.'

Although the former has given up the day job, the latter, a little stiffer of gait and more rugged of face than when he began his broadcasting career, is still at full steam in 2FM. His voice has roughened not at all. His reputation as a man who hasn't missed a beat of every pop, rock, hip hop, dance and even metal music trend is secure. Metal wouldn't be a favourite, now: 'Ah, no.' At the request of one of his daughters, he broadcast a heavy half-hour once and it wasn't successful. No. Not successful at all.

He is a widower now. His staunch Florrie died in January 2002, just weeks after Larry himself had had a heart operation. And while he has nothing but praise and love for their children and their wonderful support of him, he remains shattered at her loss. 'We never had a bad word. We were great companions.' They had been together virtually all of their lives. Having been born into the retail trade – her father ran Lucky Duffy's in Parnell Street – they met when she came to work for the Gogans in their Fairview premises.

As a couple they enjoyed simple pursuits, rambling through the streets of Dublin of an evening, window-shopping at Switzers, Weirs or Arnotts ('Of course it's no use now. That's all gone. Everything is all security and shutters, these days'), going to the pictures, having a burger or a steak afterwards somewhere nearby.

And if they weren't defying the lurching ban at the Crystal, Florrie and Larry frequently took the bus out to the Arcadia in Bray. And the bus back. It was worth the fare and the long trek. 'That was a marvellous place. They had people like Dusty Springfield.'

He misses the showbands: 'They started in the late fifties. The Clipper Carlton was the first and the four big ones in the early sixties were Dickie and the Miami, Butch and the Capitol, Eileen Reid and the Cadets, the Royal with Brendan Bowyer – they were the biggest of them all.' He has a particularly soft spot for Butch Moore: 'A lovely fella. Great voice, but really a lovely fella. They were fantastic, you know, the showbands. They gave great value for money. They put on real shows. They wore the gear and the hats and they did the moves.'

He regards Eileen Reid as a phenomenon, largely because the crowds who followed showbands up and down the country, with an enthusiasm now reserved for global rock stars, consisted primarily of women. For them, packed in around the bandstand, dancing was frequently secondary: for most of the night they screamed at the moves made by the lead singer or whichever band idol they favoured. They threw up handwritten messages and requests on scraps of paper. 'And the men came in to follow the women . . .' Eileen Reid attracted equal numbers of men and women fans. He reckons it was because of the clothes and the hairdos – 'That wedding-dress thing was marvellous.' For those too young to remember, Eileen Reid performed her major hit, a mournful ditty titled 'I Gave My Wedding Dress Away', for years in a real wedding dress, veil and all.

It is not merely the man who is a benchmark: Larry's 'Just-A-Minute' quiz has slipped into the realms of legend. A quick Google of his name will reveal blog after blog listing the bloopers made by contestants answering the quick-fire questions during the long-running feature – so long-running, in fact, that the quizmaster himself cannot always distinguish what is true from the mythical or purely made-up.

He can verify the four that follow:

'What's Gandhi's first name?'

'Goosey Goosey.'

'Where's the Great Wall?'

'Crumlin.'

'Where's the Taj Mahal?'

'Opposite the dental hospital.'

'Name the BBC's grand prix commentator.'

'Eh . . . Eh . . . Sorry—?'

'I'll give you a hint. It's something you suck . . .' The name of the commentator he had in mind was Murray Walker, and with Larry's background in sweets, the hint is to Murray mints.

The contestant hesitates for a further second or two. Light dawns: 'Oh! Yeah! Righ'! Dickie Davies!'

He has been credited with the next lot, too, but can't vouch for them all.

'What was Hitler's first name?'

'Heil.'

'Name a bird with a long neck?'

'Naomi Campbell.'

'What's the capital of France?'

'F.'

'With what town in Britain is Shakespeare associated?'

'Hamlet!'

But he's sure about these last two.

'Complete this well-known phrase: "As happy as . . ."?'

Again the contestant hesitates and Larry comes in with a rescuing hint. 'Think of me! As happy as—?'

Contestant (joyfully): 'A pig in shit!'

And this one, very un-PC but re-broadcast by his 2FM colleague, Dave Fanning, and further used by him in print to reveal the best laugh he'd had during that year:

Larry: 'What star do travellers follow?'

Contestant (instantly): 'Joe Dolan!'

All of those have become part of Dublin folklore, while the catchphrase ('Aah, they didn't suit you!'), which comforts those who fall at too many fences, has embedded itself in the city's argot. Within its compassion lies the secret of Larry Gogan's popularity. He genuinely likes people, all people, finding redeeming features in the vain and the stupid, the upstart and the arrogant. No one I have ever met has heard him speak ill of any other human being. He refuses to badmouth even those who have moved him from his regular weekday slot on 2FM to the weekend deserts – even though it is clear that he is less than happy at the dislocation and humiliated to be stopped in the streets and offered words of sympathy or disgust.

These days, particularly in the cut-throat Dublin market, broadcasting can be a bear-pit in which nice people are gobbled up. 'Nice' is frequently misused as a satirical or even pejorative term when used of people, but among other definitions my *Concise Oxford* defines it as 'kind and good-natured'. By *vox populi*, the adjective is precise where this man is concerned and may go a long way to explain why he has survived for so long at the top of his insecure profession. Perhaps there is only so much public whingeing, dirt-digging, authority-bashing and soul-searching that listeners can cope with in any twenty-four-hour period.

'Oh.' The door of the gallery above us opens and we are interrupted by two women, who are taken aback to find us occupying the studio. An apologetic 'Come in, come in, we're just finished,' from us, but then, quickly, before we turn off the tape-recorder, we do a little 'Just-A-Minute' of our own, concerning Larry's Dublin, starting with his favourite place.

Turns out it's not in Dublin city at all – but it is quite appropriate because it's the Sally Gap, up in the Dublin Mountains, from where the entire megalopolis is spread out before you like an undulating coat of many colours.

Larry's favourite Dubliner is still the late Maureen Potter, who, in his opinion, could have achieved success in any field she chose. He is correct in this assessment: as well as her public prowess in comedy, 'straight' acting, dancing, singing and film work, Potter was highly intelligent, very well organised, widely read, loved all sport but with a particular passion for cricket, and had an indefinable charisma, on and off stage, that attracted people to her. However: 'I just loved her for herself. She was so warm.'

His second favourite Dubliner is Larry Mullen of U2. 'They had some album out and I wanted to interview one of them. But I felt I wouldn't get Bono so I thought I'd ask for Larry Mullen. So I rang Chris Roche, God be good to him.'

At the time, the late Chris Roche worked in the publicity cab of the U2 juggernaut. 'You want *Larry*?' Roche couldn't believe his ears. Up to then, nobody had asked for Larry.

'Yeah. Larry. Please.'

'But no one's ever done anything with him before.'

'I want to talk to Larry.' Gogan was adamant.

'All right. I'll ask him.'

As an aside, when I interviewed Bono for the *Sunday Tribune* many years ago, he performed an hilarious impersonation of a posse of schoolgirls who, at every sighting of 'Lall-ee' during the band's tour of Japan, screamed after him in hot pursuit while ignoring the other members of the band. The other three, who had become blasé about being lionised, didn't know whether to feel slighted, or tickled pink. 'It was the blond hair. Had to be.'

In the matter of the 2FM interview with Lall-ee, our Larry didn't have long to wait. Roche was back on the line in jig time: 'He wants to know when you want him . . .' And ever after, with every album release or whatever, Larry G always got the interview with Larry M. (Once, when he was passing through Dublin airport, he was spotted by one of the juggernaut's drivers who intercepted him: 'Howya, head, I just want to tell you that Larry always says he prefers to talk to you than to *Rolling Stone* magazine.')

So that was the little cherry on top of Larry G's Christmas cake that year.

The two women are clunking down the metal gallery steps into the studio and we have to go. But he corpses with a delighted but knowing you-won't-catch-me Tinkerbell giggle on being asked one last question. Who's his favourite Dublin broadcaster?

'Terry Wogan. And he's from Limerick.'

You Can't Have a Hit without a Hough

If RTÉ harbours many whose broadcasting talents are only part of their portfolio, as in Aidan Mathews, I sometimes believe the station may not fully appreciate the width and depth of its treasures. As well as fulfilling their broadcasting commitments, its staff include not only writers, painters, philosophers, actors and musicians, both classical and popular, but the indefinable, indefatigable Kevin Hough.

Like Larry Gogan, Hough is a station lifer. But unlike Larry, whose dedication to music and broadcasting is virtually absolute, Kevin has as many facets as there are squares on a Rubik's Cube. Anyone need a singer, pianist, sound engineer, radio producer, variety artist, musical director, accompanist, actor, talent-show organiser, scriptwriter or adjudicator?

Or – oh, yes – a Buttons for your pantomime, Cinderella?

His energy is prodigious – he attributes it to 'cycling all over Crumlin' when he was a boy, delivering 'the messages' to customers of his father, who ran a grocery. He acknowledges his good luck and good health and cannot understand why, in this wonderful world, anyone could be bored: 'There just aren't enough hours in the day. But, then, we were brought up before television.'

Hough is from a large family, all of whom in the early years lived happily together in the granny's house on Beechwood Avenue, Ranelagh, and a number of whom are now singers, musicians or artists in various disciplines.

For this interview, we are again in the Radio Centre. It is still raining in the courtyard outside, but if it is true that the life a person has lived is written on his face, Kevin Hough's, round and sun-like, suggests that he has lived mostly under a benevolent sky. Even the thatch of strawberry blond hair seems to radiate light in the semi-gloom, eclipsing the faint glow from the vending machine beside where we sit in an open caboosh.

In my life, I have met only one other person whose intrinsic and infectious enthusiasm was as evident as his. He was the late Frank Patterson and, funnily enough, it transpires that the two toured America together for three months, Hough warbling baritone to Patterson's tenor and also acting as MC. Oh, to have been a supernumerary during that trip! The good cheer in the air would have been dispersed only with a JCB.

In the fifties, Hough Senior's grocery was the traditional sort, the kind that sold hardware and ham, fancies and flour, wellies, buckets, string, toothbrushes and everything any sensible resident of Crumlin could ever need – or afford. And as well as having his son to deliver the messages strapped to the back carrier of his bike, Hough Senior employed a real messenger boy, on a real messenger-boy's bike, for deliveries.

Kevin Hough's da went to the market every morning for fresh vegetables. The fish he sold on Wednesdays and Fridays came from Mortons of Ranelagh, and was a cause of friction between himself and his son: 'In those days there was no such thing as hygiene; the meat and fish were out on the counter. Flies all over it – I couldn't stand them and I'd spray all over the place and I'd kill bumblebees and everything. My father used to get really annoyed.'

His father was probably annoyed, too, at the adolescent giggling that ensued each time a customer came in to ask, 'Could I have me breast cut, please, Mr Hough?' A perfectly normal and frequent request from local housewives buying a breast cut of bacon.

And then there was the confetti. The first time he was asked for this, young Kev climbed obligingly up a ladder to fetch it: 'It was kept high on the top shelf at the back. "Fourpence ha'penny."' He gave it to the customer.

But the customer looked blankly from him to the long blue box, then back at him. That wasn't what she wanted. '*Soup* confetti,' she emphasised. Proprietor's son though he was, it then had to be explained to the kid that 'soup confetti' was what Dubliners, at least in Crumlin, called the mix of barley, lentils and dried peas they used to give body and flavour to the broth they boiled up from the free bones they got from butchers.

He also had to learn what they meant when they asked for 'them Boddery [Boudoir] biscuits', or a 'dumti' (or 'dumbtih': nobody knows how to spell it because nobody has ever seen it written down). The lah-di-dahs referred to those rubber gob-stoppers as 'soothers'. And now that you're armed with this information, try saying 'dumti' out loud and you'll get the picture.

Asked to say spontaneously what 'Dublin' means to him, Kevin Hough doesn't have to think. Theatre. Shows and show people. Actors, singers and dancers.

The Hough children, all eight, were introduced early to the joys of drama and variety. Two of their aunts, Maura and Joan O'Rourke, worked with Longford Productions at the Gate Theatre. 'There were shilling seats at the back and Lord Longford always held a row for people who wanted theatre but who were not well off. And to give him his due, he never, ever put up the price of them.'

It strikes me, by the way, that Lord Longford's concern for the 'not well off' might have extended to the plight of his wife, a thin woman with straggling hair, standing forlornly at the foot of the Gate's steps and rattling a collection box in an effort, literally, to keep the show on the road. To be fair, however, Lady Longford never seemed to mind, happily acknowledging the ha'pennies, pennies and threepenny bits of passers-by.

Anyhow, no such qualms for the Houghs in the cheap seats, chests puffed with pride and pleasure as their aunts walked about and spoke to them from behind the proscenium: 'Seeing Aunt Joan and Aunt Maura up there, it was wonderful.'

The real treat, though, was to be brought backstage afterwards. This was where drama and showbiz got into Kevin Hough's blood, never to be eradicated. 'The smells at the back of the theatre. The dust and the cracks in the floor and the greasepaint, the heat and the brightness of the lights in the dressing-room – it was all absolutely terrific.'

After the fire that ruined the theatre, the Abbey Company was into its long 'temporary' – from 1951 to 1966 – occupation of the Queen's in Pearse Street and that, too, became a Hough haunt. 'I saw *The Quare Fella* there. And that gong at the beginning of every show . . . Loved it!'

His birthday is in early January 'so it was a double treat for me because I knew that after Christmas I'd be going to the panto and there'd be the sweets and the chocolates and the cousins and all of that, and the *spectacle* . . . I'll never, ever forget *Snow White and the Seven Dwarfs* and they had a revolve on the stage. In those days? *A revolve*? In *Dublin*? They never had revolves here. You'd have to go to London for a revolve.'

The College of Music in Chatham Street is another icon. 'We were all sent there. The piano teacher was of a very nervous disposition. Don't know whether it was due to the way I played or whatever, but she had the Anadin lined up along the top of the piano and she'd start to eat them the minute I went in.' He studied the violin too, but his sister Ursula became the star violinist of the family so he left her to it: 'I was never going to fit into her shoes.'

One oul' instrument was never going to be enough for

our Kev, though, so he decided to have his voice trained and, typically, went straight to the top – to Veronica Dunne, international soprano, friend of Joan Sutherland and doyenne of Irish singing teachers, then and now. 'Ronnie's great. I stayed with her for a long time. And I learned an awful lot about diaphragm, and breathing and all of that, and I did a lot of singing in the pantomimes with Jack Cruise and so on.' And just in passing, you understand, he adds that he won two prizes in the Feis Ceoil . . .

His life in Dublin ran in circles where the same people cropped up time and time again. Aidan Mathews's Aristotelian polity?

When the granny and her extended family needed needles for the wind-up gramophone, Kevin went to May's of the Green, where he might have run into future colleagues and even my interviewees for this book – Catherine Hogan, for instance, or even Larry Gogan. He would be given his needles and, later, the sheet music for his exams, and later still, whatever comedy songs he needed for his own shows by Joan Smith, who had extensive musical knowledge. Later she worked at RTÉ as a broadcasting resource in the 'Grams Library'.

When the child Kevin had sat eating sweets in the stalls of the Theatre Royal, watching Jack Cruise in *Snow White*, did he have any intimation that he would play Buttons in Cruise's *Cinderella*?

Did he have any idea on Sunday nights when he and his family sat around the radio listening to the *Sunday Play* from the Radio Éireann Repertory Company ('We took it very seriously. And if it was a thriller, you'd be afraid to go to bed afterwards . . .') that he would one day do the sound effects for those plays in the Radio Éireann Drama Department?

And when he left his sister Ursula to her violin, did he imagine that one day he would hear her rehearsing as a member of the RTÉ Concert Orchestra in Studio One when he was just down the corridor? Or when he was watching his beloved Aunt Joan O'Rourke on stage from the Gate's cheap seats, might he have guessed he would work with her, too, when she came to preside over the costume department for RTÉ TV?

From an early age, this man juggled life, job and ambitions to be a performer. 'The R and R at the Gaiety was a big part of my life.'

The Rathmines and Rathgar Musical Society was and still is a great training ground for talented people. Professionalism without risk. 'You never got a part there unless you could project because they didn't use any mikes.' His first appearance with them was in 1963, during their fiftieth-anniversary show, 'and I directed their *Mikado* for the eightieth in 1993.' He likes the circularity of that.

If there was nothing going in the R and R, there was always work to be had in the private societies, which were perpetually engaged in a hunt for people willing, available and good enough to play lead roles. And in the case of one, nameless right now, the casting deliberations at committee level have leaked out: '*We have to have a Hough. The*

Houghs are box office, you know! You can't have a hit without a Hough.' Like a lightning bolt in reverse, the delight with which he delivers this runs from his toes to the top of his head, virtually shooting him off the seat.

His most fateful semi-professional role was in *Land of Smiles* with the Glasnevin Musical Society at the Gaiety. Unknown to him, Jack Cruise had been searching for a Buttons to appear in his Christmas panto. The late Val Fitzpatrick had seen *Land of Smiles* and told him: 'Your Buttons is round there in the Gaiety. Go to see him.'

Cruise did so and 'I got the part straight away. I didn't even have to audition. Thirteen weeks in the Olympia! I was made!'

By then he was employed as a sound man at RTÉ, but his bosses accommodated this opportunity. 'They also let me go to America in 1969 for the three months with Frank Patterson. They were really very good to me.'

Now that they've started, the anecdotes, like celebrities waiting in the wings on Oscar night, pile up to tumble out. 'That period of the sixties I would have done a lot of concerts in the Gresham. I played for my sisters who sang. The Rory O'Connor dancers were on, Ita Flynn was playing for them, God be good to her, they'd been doing a hornpipe or a jig or something, they finished up anyhow and they ran off. And someone in management ordered that they had to go on again. "Go out and do yeer heel!"

'"But we've done it!" The hapless dancers were already gasping for air.

March 1966: Nelson's Pillar minus Nelson, courtesy of the Irish Republican Army.

Broadway Cafe
advertisement.

Gresham Hotel in flames,
July 1922.

*29 June 1963: Statesman
John F. Kennedy, 35th
president of the USA,
with Dublin's macebearer,
Jim Buckley. Paddy Hanlon
was not far away.*

*Body language on the floor of
The Crystal, 1954.*

At home with Hilton and
Michael in Harcourt
Terrace, 1952.

Opposite:
Maureen Potter in
panto mode, 1989.

Moore Street, 1959.

Ha'penny Bridge and
Woollen Mills, 1949.

'"Well go out and do it again!"'

He creases at the memory. Then, wiping his eyes, launches into another, related, story. He was on tour in American with a trio of Irish dancers, two girls and a boy. 'I was twenty-six or something, the girls were only sixteen and I was to keep an eye on them. The boy was eighteen. That was an incredible tour. We went all over America, Canada, Mexico – and, anyway, we get to Niagara and we do this concert and the next morning we were all up to go to the Falls and everybody's all excited and "Isn't it *great* to be going to Niagara Falls" and I'm walking down to the falls with Maura Kelly, the harpist, and the two girls are behind us and they're wearing high heels.

'The girls are finding the going tough, giving out about the walk and the terrain. "Jays," says the first one, "me feet are killing me." They stop dead. "Let's go back to the hotel," says the other one. "What is it only water anyway!"'

In contrast to the short, sharp speech rhythms favoured by his colleague Larry Gogan, Kevin Hough talks in lengthy, looping paragraphs, speaking faster and faster as each anecdote progresses, acting it out with increasing enthusiasm and hilarity until by each punchline he and his listeners are helpless. Holding-the-sides-in-stitches-wiping-tears kind of helpless.

What follows is a story from when he appeared as the second male lead in *Jack and the Beanstalk* for Jack Cruise at the Olympia Theatre. The Beanstalk was a huge, very strong spring, coiled flat on the stage at the opening of the last scene before the intermission, to 'grow' magically so that Jack could climb up to meet the Giant, while the rest of the cast wished him farewell and good luck. That was the plan anyhow. This Jack, though, was a reluctant climber.

'My sister, Patricia, is playing the Principal Girl and we're still at the stage where the girl played the boy, and this Jack is Patty Ryan, who had won the Golden Voice of Ireland in the Royal, she's in her sixties and she has beautiful legs, lovely figure, but the voice is gone and she's talking the songs, and when we get to this climbing the Beanstalk it's "I don't want to go up the Beanstalk – I'm afraid of heights."

'And Cruise would be saying, "It's going to be all right, it's safe, I promise you, you won't fall" and she's going, "Oh, no, no, I don't want to go up the f-ing beanstalk . . ." But Jack Cruise is having none of it. She had to go up a few rungs of the Beanstalk and that was *it* and Wendy Shea had done the design – it was absolutely gorgeous, beautiful leaves – and you'd expect Jack to go up five or six feet, and we're all waving goodbye and good luck and singing "Bee-YAWND the BLU-UE Hor-AIH-zon" and we're waiting for the curtain to come down, and in those days there were two mikes on the stage and I was always next to Patty, and *every* night she used to turn round to me and [pulling a mouth-down-eyes-to-heaven grimace], "Jays, this *fuck*-ing bean-stalk . . ."'

At least she had her back to the kiddies.

In the Olympia, he performed with Jack again during the ten-week runs of *Holiday Hayride* – the summer variety counterpart to Maureen Potter's *Gaels of Laughter* at the

Gaiety – but the deal included Sunday-night shows at Butlins holiday camp in Mosney.

'Jack was funny about that. "If you can't do the Sunday night . . ." He'd leave it hanging and you knew you wouldn't get the ten-week run.

'So you went down to Butlin's for five pounds. And people stayed in Butlin's in those days for two weeks so we had to change the show every second week and we'd rehash stuff we'd done over the years, an hour or an hour and a half . . .'

They dreaded it. 'But you'd get into the car and drive down, and you'd be out singing your number and the next thing you'd hear over the loudspeaker: "BABY CRYING IN CHALET TWO THOUSAND FIVE HUNDRED AND SIXTY"' – he's laughing hard now – 'and you'd get your dinner and one of the Redcoats would say to you, "When you get the meal, don't eat the carrots because they don't wash them at all, they just throw them in . . ."'

He's creasing so much by the end of this – and so am I – that the words are lost and I have to get him to repeat it for the tape.

We calm down and rest for a few seconds.

It's the way he tells 'em.

He nominates the Olympia as his favourite theatre. 'It was magic for me, but that was in the days when they weren't allowed bring in beer and all the kind of stuff they do now. Wouldn't touch it. The smell!'

He still loves variety but believes that RTÉ has never done

justice to the genre, possibly because of a scarcity in financial resources. They're all gone now, the Royalettes and the Moonbeams at the Queens and the Bluebells at the Capitol, 'but the best of all was Dolly Sparks and Her Twelve Imps at the Olympia.'

Who?

Dolly Sparks and Her Twelve Imps. Apparently they were the precursors of the Billy Barrys.

'And Alice and Babs, of course.'

For decades Alice Dalgarno and Babs de Monte were a pair of theatrical legends in Dublin show-business circles, choreographer and costumier to the chorus lines, dragons in the matter of disciplining the girls and watching that their outfits remained pristine. And it wasn't just the girls, 'we were all watched like hawks. You couldn't sit down in your costume because it'd get creased. If they caught you you'd be fined.'

The girls were well able to talk back, however. When Hough moved on within RTÉ and was no longer available for the shows because he had to do shift work, he went back to the Olympia to see all his old friends. He found that the format of the show had changed, that a London choreographer by the name of Maxello had been hired 'and he had brought all these showgirl costumes, with huge plumes on the headpieces, and all these beaded little bustier tops, for a big walk-down at the end for the finale'.

One girl, particularly well-endowed, had difficulty with the close-fitting bodice of her costume and on the first night as, plumes tossing, she pranced down the staircase towards the front, step, *pop!*, step, *pop!*, the beads showered off with every move.

That's not the story, however.

Here's the story. After a couple of weeks, Maxello comes back to check on his creation and, backstage, this girl, still in costume, beadless, feet up, puffing a cigarette in the quick-change room at the side of the stage.

Needless to remark, on seeing her, the great man entirely loses the plot.

She doesn't move but eyes him coolly, then turns her attention to the smoke drifting slowly upwards towards the ceiling. She waits until he has blown himself out, fixes him with an accusatory stare. Then, in firm, rounded Dublin tones: 'I'll have you know that I'm after fuckin' *faint*-in!'

He has worked up to the punchline with such gusto that again we have a collapse of two stout parties in the RTÉ caboosh and it's minutes before we settle down again.

But he's on a roll.

Here's the Great Gambani 'who used to pull doves out of everywhere, his pockets and his cuffs and so on, which was terrible because I had to share a dressing room with him and his doves and he used to let the doves out between the shows and they were flying everywhere and, of course, doves are filthy. *Filthy* . . .'

He grimaces and his meaning is perfectly clear.

Then there was the tour that included the two French circus artists whose act was spinning plates on long poles.

'She would run around and he'd spin the plates. Well, we started with twenty-four plates and by the end of the tour we had only six left.'

Or the lady juggler from Liverpool, booked unseen through an agent via a catalogue, who lasted just one night. Among the articles she couldn't juggle were rubber balls, solid lifebelt-sized rings and even tennis rackets. She was game, though, and had the entire orchestra ducking for cover in the pit throughout her non-act.

During his work as a sound man, which included producing sound effects and playing the piano for Oscar Wilde's *The Importance of Being Earnest*, he got to know and love his childhood heroes from the Radio Éireann Repetory Company. 'They were all so talented. Ginette Waddell, Séamus Forde, Thomas Studley . . .'

Ginette, who lived on Merrion Square with her cats, came in one day to the studio, terribly upset. One of her females had been got at by a tom in the square. 'We all have our problems . . .' Again, he's laughing so hard he can barely speak.

As for Florence Lynch, who had a smoker's cough – 'We had to do fifty-eight takes of things' – 'She had a very old-fashioned car and she was so unhealthy she used to tie her dog to the back and drive very slowly through the Phoenix Park to exercise him.'

Kevin Hough's Dublin was larger than life, somewhat like himself.

Interestingly, like Larry Gogan, and for the same reasons,

his Dublin hero was Maureen Potter. 'With all due respect to the current crop, no one comes near her. She did her last public appearance with me as an adjudicator in the Dublin Docklands talent show in the Concert Hall. We carried her out to the taxi afterwards and that was it.'

The light dies a little, but not for long.

As so-called retirement beckons, Hough has no intention of going gardening. He is getting his ducks in a row for the Next Phase.

Hey! Is there another string to his bow? Is there anything he cannot do?

'Ah, now, listen, hold on a minute, there's a few things I can't do. Brain surgery, for instance.'

Drooling Over MacLiammóir

Kevin Hough, like Peter Sheridan and any theatre buff, gets a great kick out of the story of Mickser Reid.

Mickser, a 'short person' (he called himself a dwarf), was Jack Cruise's comic sidekick and straightman, feeding him the preambles to the gags, capitalising on the visual impact of Cruise's lankiness against his own shortness.

When the Theatre Royal was being pulled down, Mickser wasted no time in lamentations. Instead, he volunteered as teaboy to the demolition gang.

Theatre people are the ultimate pragmatists. Like Mickser, they can't afford to hold their noses over roles, or jobs, that might seem unworthy of their talents. Ya don't work, ya don't eat, head.

Yet until the advent of television, with its celebrity interviews and the tabloids' debunking of stars, the ordinary Dubliner, if there is such a person, used to regard 'theatre people' with an odd mixture of derision, tolerance, amusement, affection and awe. For even regular attendeés at the Abbey or the Gate (the houses on Thursday nights were particularly good because civil servants were paid on

Thursdays), the Eileen Crowe or Aidan Grennell they applauded on stage did not equate to the woman in a headscarf or the harassed man they saw trudging through Moore Street, juggling shopping-bags and umbrellas, or ordering tea and potatoes from a handwritten list in Liptons or Findlaters. Ah, no. It couldn't be. Rather than lessening distance, daylight mysteriously served only to compound the impression that Theatre People moved in a parallel world.

Whether they did or not, the public consciousness was that actors wore flamboyant clothes and drifted through the streets of the city with a faraway look in their eyes. Yet despite the cheap plastic raincoats and headscarves, when they travelled on steamy buses they emanated 'otherness', their lips moving as they read their scripts. They thought themselves special so everyone else thought them special too, or maybe just a little odd. Or maybe (whisper) they were all fairies.

Much of this was probably as a result of sightings, quite frequent, of Micheál MacLiammóir – or plain old "Michael" as we thesps felt entitled to call him – ambling through town in full make-up and the toupée he never removed. Ever. Even when his stage costume required him to wear a wig, he simply plonked it on top of the topper. In the Dublin of the fifties and sixties, homosexuality was rarely mentioned in public, except in a nudge-wink undertone. Mac's living arrangements in Harcourt Terrace with his partner, Hilton Edwards, were an unusual exception to the norm for same-sex liaisons.

'Maybe they were kind of accepted as street entertainment for everyone else. I don't think people really knew what they were. But maybe they half-way knew . . .' Actress Geraldine Plunkett's 'ordinary' family would have fallen into this category. 'My mother and her sister used to go to the Gate to drool over MacLiammóir.'

My own hindsight view is that Dubliners had copped on very well about who and what Hilton and Micheál were but, at that time, any deviations from the 'norm' were social undertows that, if brought to the surface, would drown us all. So, in general, we Dubs kept our thoughts to ourselves. At least, most of us did, except on the very rare occasions when one of these fairies was blatantly taking up our space or breathing our very oxygen, and really getting on our wick.

Such as the time I was sitting in Neary's pub on a rainy weekday afternoon and was witness to such an affront. The pub was almost empty but at one end of the counter sat Mac, fully made-up and toupéed as usual. Apparently unaware that, from the far end of the bar, he was the recipient of increasingly poisonous glares from a pint-swilling Dub, he was quiet, sipping a drink and, somewhat ostentatiously, minding his own business. Actually, he was radiating minding-his-own-business, acting it, just as he would on stage.

Having failed to provoke a reaction, the Dub, finally, could no longer contain himself: 'Aah, for God's sake why don't yerself and Hilton get effin' married?'

'We can't.' Quick as a flash. MacLiammóir had not even

glanced in the Dub's direction. 'We're Catholics!'

The Dub retired.

Geraldine Plunkett's mother was presented with a dilemma when, unexpectedly, after an audition for Earnán De Blaghd at the Abbey, her daughter was offered the chance to become part of the theatre milieu in which These People moved. Suddenly, she had perforce to move from the 'half-know' category to the 'need-to-know'.

Never mind that the whole family were regular theatregoers. That no longer counted. Watching and enjoying plays, drooling over handsome actors, was a different proposition from putting your daughter on the stage, Mrs Worthington.

Mrs Plunkett had met her husband when they both worked in Dunlops and, as 'straightforward Catholics', had embarked with him on giving their family a simple upbringing. Geraldine's activities in the school holidays involved playing tennis at the local club or going to the pictures.

Faced with this decision about her daughter, the mother called an urgent family meeting. 'She was the eldest but she was a widow by then and felt she should consult. So she met with the brothers to decide how to proceed.'

It was a galvanising offer. After school, the young Geraldine had gone to work in Hallmark Cards. 'In my innocence I thought I'd be writing verses and so on.' Instead she found herself on an assembly line, folding thin sheets of cardboard and adding glitter. She mimes the work, hands and arms flashing forwards and back: 'Glitter-fold-glitter-fold-glitter-glitter-*glitter* . . . ' The chance to join a distinguished actress roster, which included May Craig, Eileen Crowe, Aideen O'Kelly, Máire Ni Dhómhnaill and Angela Newman, presented a pretty exciting alternative. However, she would have gone along with her mother's wishes.

'Well, Phyllis . . .' After much discussion, the brothers came to the conclusion that 'It'll probably be all right. It's the Abbey. At least it's not the Gate!' The implication being, of course, that the Gate was suffused by this Hilton-and-Micheál 'thing'. Whatever it was. Wasn't wholesome anyhow.

And leaving the 'thing' aside, didn't the Gate put on plays involving women wearing nothing but seven veils – *and then taking them off*? God alone knew what people who worked in that place got up to when the curtain came down.

The Abbey, though, was different. Didn't they put on plays with titles like *The Rugged Cross* and *The Country Boy* and *The Evidence I Shall Give*? And if they did showcase bad language and out-of-wedlock pregnancy in *Juno and the Paycock*, that was only O'Casey being realistic about those northside tenements.

There was Brendan Behan's *The Quare Fella*, but sure we all had to move with the times, didn't we? And Mountjoy was another northside institution. It wasn't in your face. 'They thought the Abbey would be like its plays.' The actress, mother of seven with her husband, the actor and artist Peadar Lamb, whom she met in the Abbey, is very beautiful when she smiles.

We are speaking in the lobby lounge of the Gresham Hotel. It is lunchtime so the place is noisy and crowded. 'God bless us. If they'd only known what was going on in there!' The smile dissolves into a fit of giggles, and if the smile was infectious, the giggling infuses the air around us with mischievous delight: 'I was as green as grass when I went into the Abbey. I was shocked at all the goings-on.'

Of course she was shocked. Having had such a sheltered upbringing, she had had no idea of the absolute and burning necessity for the moral strictures then pertaining, as issued by the formidable Archbishop John McQuaid of Dublin. The fact that the grateful leaders of Ireland customarily knelt to kiss his ring, or that squads of librarians had to engage themselves in obscuring, if not excising, 'immoral' passages in library books, had never crossed her radar. If it had, she would have been grateful; if we hadn't had such moral leaders, we'd have been wallowing in bawdy filth as our ancestors did in the Brehon days. 'I'd no reason to know. There was no reason for me to be aware of anything. Maybe I was repressed and didn't know it!'

So what did Phyllis's daughter see when she entered the Abbey Theatre at the Queens? What goings-on could have torn the scales from her eyes?

Her lips are sealed. And so are mine.

Wha'?

Poor Phyllis Plunkett didn't know the half of what was going on in Dublin theatre circles where Cecil Sheridan was a legendary comic and popular panto dame. This next story, in which the Queen's Theatre has a walk-on, is again courtesy of Peter Sheridan (no relation) via Cecil's son, the artist Noel Sheridan, also, sadly, no longer with us.

Noel is about fifteen and the mother is out of her mind with worry: 'You're out of control, you're smoking and you're drinking and you're going out with girls – and I've lost total control of you.

'So you're going to go down now to your father. He has something he wants to say to you. You're going to go down to that Queen's Theatre right now and you're going to talk to your father.'

So Noel goes down to the father, down to the Queen's Theatre.

He goes in the stage door. 'Where's me father?'

'He's in dressing room number one.'

Son goes into the bowels of the theatre, opens the door of the dressing room and there's a man sitting, legs spread, fishnet tights on, skirt up to kingdom come, false tits and a wig, and he's wagging his finger at his son: 'Yew are fucking breaking your mother's heart . . .'

No Standing in the Upper Saloon

Nothing that happens among Theatre People would shock Bernard Farrell: he's been living with them since he left the day job at Sealink twenty-one plays ago.

It is customary for interviewers to characterise him as 'everybody's favourite dinner-party guest', certainly as someone who is perpetually in good humour, always a pal, always ready with the funny, as opposed to O'Casey's 'bitther', word. He remains blithe even about those who dismiss his drama as 'slight'.

From time to time he is damned with the faint praise that his work is 'very well constructed'– in an era when this is no longer *à la mode*. And anyway, for God's sake, isn't it true that his plays exhibit no 'bite' and lack 'edge'? Translation: no conspicuous horror, violence, cerebral gymnastics, scatological language or obvious physical abuse.

I am sure this hurts but he shrugs it off: 'Shocking people in the theatre is easy. A torture scene is easy.'

His real answer, which he does not trumpet, is the increasing amount of time he spends travelling all over the world attending his openings in Europe, America, Canada and Australia. There was even a production of *I Do Not Like Thee, Doctor Fell* in South Korea – and, would you believe? – in Vatican City with an all-male cast, while both *Stella By Starlight* and *Lovers of Versailles* have been produced in Sydney, one at the Sydney Opera House, no less.

His plays may be funny in parts and gentle overall, but they are neither potboiler nor slight. Audiences might rock with merriment at the way he writes about Dubliners with such affectionate glee. But as they leave the theatres their skin is prickling with recognition of pretension, class snobbery, alienation from a society increasingly intent on 'achievement', schoolroom bullying, the stress of a put-upon wife, or a family's impatience with and neglect of aged relatives.

No 'bite', huh?

So, this public bonhomie cloaks a deeply serious man. Except for brief flashes, noticed only by those watching for them, it is likely that no one except his wife, Gloria, sees this side of him. In company, his expression is open, inviting friendship and confidences.

We are talking in Toddy's Bar, the least posh part of the Gresham's lobby lounge. Our fellow guests sneak the odd look at him: they have seen him somewhere, they have heard him somewhere – but where? Who is he? If he notices the covert surveillance, he does not betray it. He certainly does not invite it. Bernard is a watcher.

Very early in life, like all writers, he fell in love with words. 'Pusillanimous', anyone? 'Serendipitous'?

113

'Dyspraxia'? 'Congruence'? It's not only the images they engender, it's the sound. We just love the way those onomatopoeic syllables roll moistly around the tongue and teeth.

For Farrell, one of the very earliest delights was to discover, displayed on his local bus (and still current) the immortal legend: 'No Standing In The Upper Saloon.' 'It's great, isn't it?'

Only a word-gourmet or gourmand would appreciate its incongruity. On the surface, it seems absurd to apply the phrase 'Upper Saloon' – implying the lounge of a Mississippi riverboat in all its shining hardwood and brass splendour – to the top deck of what was in our youth a jerky, noisy bone-shaker, its expletive-laden air misty with cigarette smoke and steam from wet serge. And although it is likely to have been presented from the factory already fixed to the staircase of the vehicle, in Farrell's mind that exhortation had to have been the product of a romantic, a dreamer who lived for Saturday picture matinées where he cheered on the chap in the follyer-uppers.

'I feel the loss of Old Dublin, I really do. There was a pace then, a slowness. The clip-clop of the horses and rumble of the trams, and your da saying, "Mind the manure when you're walking across O'Connell Street."

'There was poverty, sure, and beggars, and fellas going around with one leg and trousers pinned up and a crutch. But it was very safe. I really don't think that was a cliché. The kind of poverty you see now is baseball-cap poverty –

people out of their skulls – and when I read that people get kicked in the head . . .

'Back then if you got into fights you didn't kick anyone. And if someone fell on the ground, the fight just stopped.' He is running a one-man protest to reclaim the boardwalk along the Liffey that, despite the best efforts of many, has been colonised by drug-dealers and their unfortunate clients. Every time he comes into the city centre, he makes a point of using it: 'I'm trying to do my bit, but the cokeheads there are very aggressive.'

To get back to the past, Bernard might be tinged with the romanticism exhibited by the author of the 'saloon' conceit. For instance, he endows the typical Dublin woman of his youth with Junoesque qualities: 'I remember them as being very big whereas the men were skinny.' Like all writers, he quests, burrows and compares: 'When we see O'Casey on the stage, we recognise authenticity.' He is in a position to know this. As a young man, he worked for a while in an estate agency, where part of his job entailed doing the rounds with a rent collector, whose beat included ex-tenements converted into 'private flats' in places like Dorset Street, *bona fide* O'Casey territory. 'We collected from a whole block there and another block down on Arran Quay.'

This rent collector, a man called McGowan, warned him before they went into the first flat that he was not to touch anything. 'I thought he meant "don't rob anything" and I was offended.'

The two men were greeted with courtesy and even

jolliness – but it was hard for Bernard to believe they had not stepped on to a set. 'It was all there. Just this one big room with a curtain across it. And in the bedroom part there was the old man in the bed.' Seumus Shields, *Shadow of a Gunman*. 'So we spoke to this man in the bed and all that,' and the woman of the house produced the rent book and the money and it was marked up, 'and I was standing there, taking it all in, and then, forgetting the instructions not to touch anything, I put my hand on a chair and the chair collapsed.'

The warning had sprung from the rent collector's humanity. 'He knew that while the furniture was falling to pieces, on rent day they would arrange it so it would look as though it was OK.' Then there would be no report that tenants were 'wrecking the place', which would have led to serious consequences, even eviction.

Farrell's recall of pastimes – making badges by removing the cork from inside bottle caps, putting it inside your shirt and snapping the metal back on through the fabric – street games, monikers and food of his youth in Dun Laoghaire and Dublin is secure. 'Whereas poshies enjoyed "dessert" after their dinners, people like us were served "sweet". We had tapioca [frog spawn] semolina, stewed apple, rhubarb or gur cake – a heavy, sickly sweet concoction, topped with pastry and constructed from stale bread soaked in black tea, raisins, currants and lots and lots of sugar. If your ma didn't make it, it could be bought by the slice in your local grocer's.

'For high holidays we had tinned peaches, or maybe even

pears, although they weren't such a good idea because sometimes there were only three pear halves in the tin. That would be grand in a family, of, say, six, half a pear each, but unhappy differences arose in families whose numbers were not divisible by three. Mothers in families of four, for instance, had a terrible time trying to create four equal portions out of three very slippy and syrupy halved pears, resulting inevitably in cries of "She got more than me." We poured Bird's custard over the lot.'

From memory, Bernard admires the skill and speed with which butter was carved from blocks, slapped on marble scales, which had brass weights, then shaped with wooden paddles and parcelled up in greaseproof paper. (I was particularly fascinated by the dairy custom of 'the cat's tilly', the extra few drops added to the milk ladled into customers' jugs.)

Where epithets were concerned, in the days when these were merely cleveralities and not a source of serious insult, he reveals that '"a ninety-nine in the shade" was a "hot" woman; a "haloosh" was a loose one; a hacker meant "she'll do".'

Hey! Don't blame the messenger. We're talking about times when for Christmas presents Moore Street traders were wont to yell at us to 'get the last of the Baluba Babies', alongside our Cheeky Charlies, and on putting pennies into mission collection boxes in school or at church, we were thanked by the nodding plastic head of an Official Black Baby.

Back then, just as butter was cut from golden blocks, so

117

was soap apportioned: black for floors, red carbolic for general washing, Sunlight for delicates and bathtime, 'and wouldja give us a ball of blue and a packet of Red Robin?' Reckitt's Blue, to whiten the shirts and sheets, came in hard little balls in an astonishingly vivid shade of indigo. The Red Robin starch was for collars, cuffs and dickeys – false shirt fronts to wear under your jacket when you hadn't a clean shirt, or any shirt at all:

> Janey Mac,
> Me shirt is black,
> What'll I do for Sunday?
> Go to bed,
> And cover your head,
> And don't get up 'till Monday!

The chants that accompanied street games were intimately wound in with daily life. During my own childhood, detergent was becoming available but it was comparatively very expensive. I knew all about it, though: while minding my own business in the roadways around Ballymun I was frequently jeered with catcalls of 'Persil washes whiter!' Persil's rival, Rinso, was used to regulate the rhythmic bouncing of a rubber ball against a wall, with appropriate actions. 'Plainy' was an underhand throw, 'over' was overhand, 'downy' hit the ground before it hit the wall, 'right leg' was bounced under it and so on:

> Plainy packet of Rinso,

Over packet of Rinso,
Downy packet of Rinso,
Dashy packet of Rinso,
Right leg packet of Rinso,
Left leg packet of Rinso,
Backy packet of Rinso . . .

When a blouse or cotton dress became too fragile for bleach and starch, because of its repeated punishment against the washboard, the remedy was a vial of Drummer Dye. In black, it was used when a bereaved woman could not afford a new black wardrobe for her year of mourning. Men got away with black ties, armbands and diamonds sewn into the sleeves of their jackets or jumpers.

Farrell becomes reflective. 'I don't see many of these games, these days. Nobody has slingshots any more, or spinning tops with those leather whips, or hoops [played simply by bowling the bare rim of a wheel along the roads]. Nobody is now categorised by being either a *Beano* or a *Dandy* aficionado, whether your fave was Keyhole Kate or Minnie the Minx, and remember Lord Snooty and his Posh Pals?'

I do. I remember the top hat Lord Snooty wore. I also remember 'knick knack', when you rang the doorbell of a cranky neighbour and ran away, risking identification or even capture.

That is still extant, I think, but nobody now plays Broken Statues: 'You stood in a line, someone came to you, spun you around and cast you away. You stumbled and whatever way you ended up you had to freeze and couldn't move.'

There was one game he thinks peculiar to Dun Laoghaire, called Dab. It was played by two boys. Each of us threw a coin against a wall and the boy whose coin landed closest to it became the Killer. The victim had to throw his coin as far as possible; the Killer aimed for it with his own. If he hit it, he could claim it.

Of course, in Ballymun we didn't have coins to throw around like that. *We* had to play One Potato, for which we all stood close together while one after the other, fists were thumped on fists to make a tower.

One potato,
Two potato,
Three potato,
Four,
Five potato,
Six potato,
Seven potato,
More!

The ultimate purpose was to have your fist at the top by the end of the chant.

Trips into Dublin for Bernard Farrell and his family were frequent, to shop, of course, to attend theatres – 'When other families were going to the pictures, we were going to plays' – to go to Adam and Eve's in Merchant's Quay for the Blessing of the Throats on St Blaise's Day. This was such a popular event that street traders set up shop along the route, offering their specialised wares – 'Olive oil or flannel!' My mother and grandmother always swore that red flannel, it had to be red, was the business for easing colds and chest infections.

Easter brought the Farrells into O'Connell Street for the Military Parade, over which the 'flypast' was short, but exciting. Unless you missed it because you were adjusting a sock.

And on Saturdays, at the far side of the Ha'penny Bridge, Bernard liked to stand in the little plaza beside the Woollen Mills, which proclaimed in its window that 'This shop has nothing to do with the shop next door.' The place buzzed with sword swallowers, fireaters and jugglers – I even saw a snake charmer there once. Biggest attraction of all was the stall set up by Hector Grey, the man who introduced the words 'Made in Hong Kong' to the Dublin huckster marketplace.

The future playwright's attention, though, was usually drawn to the three-card-trick merchant, so often 'that I got to know the cohorts and lookouts', the 'plants' who would materialise from the crowd to 'win' against the trickster and thereby prove the game was legitimate.

The city was playground, school and theatre, but as he got older, and interested in girls, he avoided the corner of Dame Street and South Great George's Street, where the Sign of the Baldie, hairs rising from his head in neon strings (it's still there) flashed accusingly at him. Follically challenged from a young age as he thought he was, 'I was very sensitive and if I was going out with a girl I'd steer clear of that!'

The real highlight, though, was the annual visit to Santa at Clerys when, depending on the state of the family finances, either a blue or a pink ticket was bought. Nothing to do with sex: the colour of the ticket denoted how much was paid for it and the resultant value of Santa's present, whether it would be a cheap cardboard kaleidoscope or a ritzy, 360-piece jigsaw of a thatched English pub. The present might even be a Jew's harp 'that'd knock your teeth out'. With a finger he makes plucking gestures at the side of his mouth, 'G'dhoyng-g'dhoyng-g'dhoyng . . .'

The Holy Grail was a gun with a roll of caps to play Cowboys and Indians, 'and a holster. You used to turn the holster around the wrong way so you could draw to the front. Foxing the other fella. If you hadn't a gun, you'd use a hurley for a rifle, or the branch of a tree, and you'd be riding into town, slapping your own behind as though it was the horse's behind . . . You really believed it. You could see the horse. You were slapping a real horse's behind. The imagination was wonderful.'

But, of course, somebody's pesky little sister would always want to join in. Down, girl! Back in the saloon where you belong . . .

One of those Clerys Santa visits still haunts him. 'I went in and I had a blue ticket. And there was a woman who took the ticket, and she murmured, "Blue ticket," to Santa.'

He went up to Santa who smiled at him. 'Have you been a good boy?'

'"Yeah, Santa. I've been a good boy."

'And Santa reached up the chimney and he took down the wrapped parcel. "Now be a good boy and have a nice Christmas." And he handed it to me.'

But the woman murmured, a warning, '"Santa, he had a blue ticket . . ." So he took the parcel back from me and he shouted up the chimney, "Blue ticket," and another parcel came down and he gave it to me: "There y'are."

'And I got the Mickey Mouse parcel.'

In *front* of everybody . . .

It is probable that little Bernard Farrell left Santa's grotto with his head held high and, for the benefit of anyone watching, a deliberate pep in his step. Deadly.

Radio Dinners

Like Kevin Hough, myself and many others, Bernard Farrell underlined the impact of radio, Din Joe and his Rory O'Connor dancers, the *Sunday Play*, the *Irish Hospital Sweepstakes Programme* with Ian Priestley Mitchell . . .

For me, the word 'wireless' still prompts associations of certain foods with certain programmes. Dinnertime on Sundays was Ciarán Mac Mathúna with bacon and mushy peas, followed by stewed apple (or jelly) with Bird's custard. We listened to his closing signature tune with a cup of Nescafé spooned from a tiny round tin and made with hot milk. This was a once-a-week treat.

Saturday's dinner was a pot-pourri of whatever food was available after the week, along with Charlie McGee and his gay guitar on the Waltons' programme.

We had shepherd's pie on Monday, stew on Thursday, fish and chips on Friday, variously accompanied by exhortations to buy stuff – stockings from Bradmola or Sunbeam Wolsey – or to send our cleaning to Prescott's.

We had the daily *Kennedys of Castleross*, with Marie Keane as Mrs Kennedy, whose reaction to any crisis in the life of her wayward son, Christy, was always to make a cup of tea. The long-running *Kennedys* gave employment to many actors, including those – Ms Keane, Vincent Dowling, Angela Newman, Philip O'Flynn, Aideen O'Kelly, Pat Laffan, Bill Foley and Eddie Golden – I later met when I joined the Abbey Theatre. I even got to sit in on a few recordings, while nurturing an ambition to be one of the characters. Never made it, though . . .

In those days Radio Éireann boasted ladys presenters with euphonious names Melosina Lenox Conyngham, Petronella: O'Flanagan, to name two. On hearing them, I repeated their names out loud and always imagined they wore hats.

Ms O'Flanagan, who presented *Between Ourselves* for women listeners, came to broadcasting in 1953, having written a regular column in the *Irish Independent* called 'Woman's Parade'. The programme, a magazine miscellany, was complementary to her column, even a development of it. Initially it was aired on Thursday evenings from between eight forty-five and nine-thirty – presumably when it was felt that housewifely duties had been completed, the cocoa was steaming gently in the hand, and the men were safely in the shed, planing wood.

An Encounter with Four Young Gentlemen

I discovered early on that we Catholics were not the only kids in town. 'Why can't you be more like Jean Brooks?' was the perpetual cry from my mother about my first best friend who lived on the other side of Dean Swift Road in Ballymun. It is because of this, I think, that to this day I believe subconsciously that Protestants are 'gooder' than Catholics.

Les Coleman recognises the concept but, like me, cannot articulate exactly why. From a working-class background, he was brought up amongst Catholics in Cameron Square, an enclave of forty-eight houses in the vicinity of Kilmainham, Mount Brown and Inchicore, entered on one side by a small roadway, on the other by a stone stairway of fifty-two steps. 'I think there was that feeling all right amongst our neighbours. We weren't really different from any of them, but my ma was looked up to. To them she was a lady. For no particular reason, only because she was a Protestant. It's a silly thing but it's just the way it was. There was a misconception that Protestants couldn't be working class, but Cameron Square was owned by the Society for

Housing the Poor, and we weren't the only Protestants in it. There were ten families. We all rented.'

Les is a big, happy-faced man who, if this does not sound too peculiar, perfectly fills his skin while sitting at ease in the house in Artane he shares with his wife, Pat. His father was a shop-fitter and carpenter, among those who built the monumental altar on O'Connell Bridge for the Eucharistic Congress in 1932 – after which he never ceased talking about the wonder of its construction. 'I've been hearing about the Eucharistic Congress all my life, but all that really mattered to him at the time was that he got paid!'

Growing up, Les played with 'all the kids on the road but I was always taller and anyone who called me a Proddy got a belt in the face. That was the rule and they knew that!'

Most of his leisure activities, however, took place within reach of his church. Boys' Brigade filled most evenings: Monday was gym, Tuesday was band practice, for which he played the cornet and became so proficient that he was co-opted into the Steadfast Brass Band. Wednesday was first aid and rugby training, Thursday was parade, drilling in full uniform, and Saturday was band practice again or rugby. 'You were with all your pals all the time. I loved Boys Brigade.'

Sundays were devout. 'After Sunday school you went to church, then to Boys' Brigade Bible class and then, if you weren't very lucky, you'd go to church again that night.'

In the larger community, we are sometimes inclined to believe that our prejudices against those outside our own grouping have to be watched, but they work in reverse too. The Brigade had a function other than entertainment. By filling their time enjoyably, it protected those lads, who were between twelve and eighteen, from the wiles of girls. 'And, of course, it segregated us from Catholics, kept us safe.'

With all this activity in the evenings, what about his schoolwork?

'That's why I'm only a carpenter!'

He served his time with his da. 'Never wanted to be a carpenter. Didn't want to be a carpenter. Always told I was going to be a carpenter. My brother went to Mountjoy school and left early, and in our house he was always "just a clerk", so for me it was "You're going to go into a trade and that's that."'

It never occurred to him that he could 'be' anything else – although there might have been a window of opportunity early on. 'Someone came in from Guinness's to our school to ask our class how many of us had fathers working with the company.' Les, of course, couldn't put up his hand. But he might have, and maybe an exception would have been made. Like Jameson's, Guinness's, as most Dubliners accepted, hired mainly Protestants.

However, carpentry it was, and no arguments. He started at fourteen. 'About a week after I left school, I was lying in bed one morning and my da said, "Come on, you're coming into work with me," and that was that.' Les has been working as a carpenter ever since.

Although he was asked to stay on as a warrant officer –

organiser – in the Boys' Brigade when he got to the age of eighteen, he had had enough: 'I had discovered girls.'

'Discovering girls' was another activity that was closely watched. You never went to a public dance-hall: that would be a euphemism for "open to all". 'George's here, where the church is, that was a great dance to go to or King's Hospital in Blackhall Place.' King's had a particular attraction: 'It was a school, and the tuck shop was on the other side of the rugby pitch, so a lot could happen on the dark way over to get a mineral!'

Pat prompts him: 'And there was the Molesworth Hall.'

'Yeah. They're all gone now.'

A dance-goer was never directly asked at the door of a hall to declare his or her religious allegiance, 'except in the Memorial Hall in Rathfarnham. That was very strict. They'd ask you outright.' The opposite was the case at the door of the Sandford parish hall in Ranelagh: 'You felt really adventurous going there because they didn't care what you were.'

Your ma always cared, though. 'If I went out with a girl, she always asked if the girl was Protestant – and, of course, whether she was or she wasn't the answer was always "Yeah."'

Pat's Clontarf family had the same interest in segregating their daughter from harm: 'It was always "Go to your own dances."'

If they ventured into a mixed dance, were they conscious of who was what? Were Catholics exotic?

'Sort of. The odd time you would sneak into the Crystal or the Metropole.

'That's another thing . . .' The memories are crowding and they look at one another as they recall Christmas Eve at the Metropole, the afternoon dance. 'For some reason,' this is Les again, 'all the Protestants in Dublin would find themselves there, not intentionally or by design, and that was great because you were dancing in a public dance-hall and we'd all end up in the Theatre Royal that night.'

There was a live show in the Royal on Christmas Eve?

'Oh, yes. Film and variety show. And the attendance that night was at least fifty per cent Protestant for the film and the show. This would have been the mid-fifties.'

The extent to which Les's parents were protective of their minority status came to the fore when his brother married a Catholic. 'He worked in Raleigh on Hanover Quay. He met her in work and they started going together. There was ructions in our house. From particularly my ma.'

It was not just words either: 'He had to move out of the house and go to England.'

'He was put out.' This is from Pat.

'Yes. He was put out. None of us was at the wedding.'

The house was two-up-two-down and the parlour doubled as Les's bedroom. Above his head, night after night, he could hear his mother's sobs. 'But they wouldn't relent.'

Oddly, his mother did not seem to mind that Les accompanied his Catholic pals on Holy Thursday when they 'did' the 'Seven Chapels' to secure a Plenary Indulgence for themselves. They cheated. They usually 'did' St Michaels in Inchicore maybe three times, but then they'd go down to St James's, John's Lane and St Audoen's in High Street, he forgets where else. He didn't know what the 'doing' meant. 'I hadn't a clue. I'd just sit at the back waiting for them to hurry up.'

In Ireland, generally, there is an ill-concealed gossipy interest in the British royal family, an interest, it might be assumed, that would be keener among those whose (very distant) antecedents arrived from across the water. Yet another shibboleth. 'Not really,' says Pat.

They can think of no one in their circle whose interest in the Royals was more unusually intense than the general run of the country. Except Les's sister. 'Tell her about Rita,' Pat prompts again.

From an early age, this sister, Rita was 'mad about the royals. So much so that for her twenty-first birthday present, my ma and da brought her over to the Coronation.'

Next thing, Rita got herself a job in Buckingham Palace as a housemaid. She was given her own apartment there, brought her Irish relatives on tours of the place when they went over: 'The Gold Room, the Silver Room, the *weight* of that stuff!' This is Pat, the long-time recipient of all the news from the Palace when Rita telephoned home to talk to her brother. Her favourite, they learned, was Prince Charles who, as a small boy, would apparently wander into the kitchen to eat bread and jam with the servants.

One of the perks of Rita's job was that tickets the royals

themselves couldn't or wouldn't use were passed on to staff – the Royal Box at Ascot, the Royal Albert Hall, Rita went to them all. And Pat went as Rita's guest to the staff ball at the Palace.

'All the royal family make it their business to attend it. Diana was in Germany with the troops, though, and wasn't expected back. There was Joe Loss in one room, another top band in another . . . We were all put into this huge state room and all lined up, and these huge doors opened and the Royal Family arrived, the Queen, and Philip and Charles, and Fergie and Andrew and Princess Anne, they were all there. And Diana too. She got back in time. She had made it her business to get back for it.' Pat gives an approving nod.

So did they say anything, these Royals? As they passed the line?

'Nothing to report there, alas! "Don't speak to them," Rita told me, "just dip your left leg."' So Pat did. And continued to admire, in particular, the staff from the Royal Yacht in full dress uniform 'and the Balmoral crowd, all the different royal households represented. The style was fabulous. I came out of that Palace with my mouth hanging open.'

The sole disappointment was the fare on offer. 'To tell you the truth I wasn't all that impressed with the food. Just rice and chicken.'

Rita, now retired, lives snugly in Old Windsor in a two-bedroom apartment the Royals gave her. 'It's lovely, isn't it, Les?'

He agrees.

As churchgoers, they give time to their faith. Les is on the Select Vestry, the management committee that runs the finances of the parish; he is also one of two glebe wardens, responsible for maintenance and upkeep of the rectory. Pat is on the church flower rota and the cleaning rota, taking her turn once a month. And she is a member of the Mothers' Union, a worldwide voluntary organisation: 'We do as much good as we can.'

Neither is conscious of having suffered any discrimination. The special standing of the Roman Catholic Church in the Irish Constitution 'never bothered Les. 'I like being a little bit different. A bit unique.'

Outside Cameron Square, though, there were a few tribal matters. Coleman attended St James' National School, 'and I had to pass Rialto School to get to mine. I never walked. I always ran. You'd be bashed. But, of course, if we caught one of them near our school, we'd do the same to them. Anyway, this day about three or four of them caught me and dragged me to stand me up against a wall. I was about nine.'

They held their threatening faces close to his. 'Do you believe in the Blessed Virgin Mary?'

'All I had to say was, "yes," but, of course, like a fool, I thought, If they believe in it, I shouldn't believe in it, so I said, "No."'

Whap!

And then they let him go.

'But they were gentlemen. They took off my glasses before they hit me.'

Chair of Chairs

Like Les and Pat Coleman, Karen Erwin belongs to the Church of Ireland and, like them, was conscious when she was growing up that she was a Protestant rock in a sea of shifting Catholics. She found it of no huge import in her day-to-day life.

Admittedly in her early days she, like the Colemans, spent her time among her co-religionists. She, too, went to Sunday School. She was a Girl Guide, and underwent Protestant schooling at Alexandra College, but her background could not be more different from theirs. She comes from a comfortably off family, and lives in the home in which she was brought up – a wonderful old house behind high walls and with easy access to the foothills of the Dublin Mountains.

She personifies a living litany of multiple achievements and leadership.

Chair of the Equality Authority.

Pray for us.

Chair of the Irish Auditing and Accounting Supervisory Authority.

Pray for us.

Chair of St Columba's College Board of Management.

Pray for us.

Chair of the Chairperson's Forum, comprising Chairs of State bodies, i.e. Chair of Chairs.

Pray for us.

Amen.

She is a president too.

Former president of the International Women's Forum (IWF) Ireland, the Irish branch of a worldwide peer association formed to support women 'at the top' and to promote leadership among those who aspire to it.

President of the Mediators' Institute of Ireland, because her day job now is as a professional mediator, via fifteen years as a litigation partner in A&L Goodbody and eight as an executive director of the *Irish Times*. She is also an 'ordinary' non-executive member of the Irish Heart Foundation Board.

That is who she is on paper, but it is not who Karen Erwin is in reality.

With her (natural, dammit!) blonde hair cropped to chin length, she is a working mother whose life is dedicated to her two boys, her husband and her elderly dad. Somehow she manages to mind the family and all the bodies she belongs to. She also practises daily what the IWF preaches: to give support and encouragement to women with potential to change the world. She is currently mentoring twenty of them.

She travels widely for stimulation and to learn about other cultures. She is usually the first to throw herself into mastering the intricacies of whatever dance craze is current at parties. And – oh, yes – she got fed up with Dublin traffic so she now travels on a motorbike, wearing leathers, the whole shebang.

Why, then, is she included in a book that seems preponderantly to concentrate on those whose Dublin past is filled with trade or service and/or a shared experience of making-do through hard times?

Well, Karen is as much of a Dub as any of us. In particular, a Dub who attended Dublin University, that walled city-within-a-city on College Green.

The college received its charter from Queen Elizabeth I in 1592. Ironically, considering it was meant for the education of the Protestant Ascendancy, it was set up on the grounds of All Hallows, an old monastery. Along the way, it suffered its own hardships: for example in 1641, when the pesky native Irish were acting up again – just as our rulers were distracted by a bit of internal bother in England – things got so bad that the provost had to flee, the college fell into disarray and, a couple of years later, had to pawn its valuable plate.

It was a few years – until 1904 – before women were considered intelligent enough to be allowed in, and the next huge upheaval was when, after Partition, the university found itself outside the United Kingdom. Sensibly, it adapted.

Our heroine signed on in 1968. 'As soon as I walked through Front Gate – I know it's a cliché – I felt I was coming home.'

Translation: I walked through Front Gate. I surveyed the crowds of students in Front Square. All those poor little lambs wandering aimlessly around, no one to marshal them, the pets . . .

So, at the age of seventeen, Karen McDowell, as she was then, set to, and before she had finished her four-year primary degree in English, psychology and history of art, there was hardly anyone on campus with whom she was not at least on nodding acquaintance. Piece of cake. There were only four thousand students to get to know. (It might be a little more difficult now – at last count, Trinity had 15,500 on its roll.)

Her nodding acquaintanceships included the staff, because she was the first student to take a seat on one of the internal administrative boards alongside the authorities: 'Can't remember the title of it but it was a great stride forward.'

It's the striding, d'you see? That's the point. The leading . . .

It wasn't all striding, however, it was throwing too. She became so good at judo, gaining college colours in the sport, that she had to give it up. 'The judo people wanted me to do nothing else except judo one hundred per cent of the time.'

And she had much else to do. Like run the Elizabethan Society.

The wha', Gay?

The Elizabethan Society, based in 'number six', a room

above the entrance arch. Probably named after you-know-who, the one with the red wig and the ruff round her neck. Karen had to become president of that.

But what did the ES, as she calls it, actually do?

'We provided lockers and sitting rooms and places for women to study. That was necessary when women weren't afforded any of those things, any facilities.' Including rooms. Living in was not for lady students until 1972. 'Oh, yes, politics, college politics with a small 'p', was always the big discussion item. Very overblown.'

The students who hung around Front Square or partook of food in Commons over the years included Wolfe Tone and Henry Grattan, Dean Swift, Edmund Burke and Oliver Goldsmith. They, we may presume, were involved in big 'P' discussion groups and Karen was aware of *some* such debates and argy-bargys in her time but not of much significance. 'For instance, there were Red Commies and internationalists there, and a few other such groups, highly vocal but not very numerous.' She didn't engage much with *their* concepts, thank you very much, because philosophically, as must be obvious by now, this woman is not drawn to agitation and causes, but to getting stuck in. To solve. To sort. So little time, so many groups to join, concerts to organise: 'I ran Human Need Week – it was for the Third World and local issues, collected money from events and so forth . . .'

'Commons' is the term used for a communal meal taken in Trinity's dining hall. It is free to scholars and some others, available to everyone else by paid ticket. A lot of ritual attaches to Commons. Gowns are obligatory. The summons is by campus bell at six – 'One of my standard memories is of hearing the bell and then seeing all of these black gowns flying across the square as people ran. You got a small Pyrex glass of porter and the doors were locked at six-thirty. If you weren't in, tough.' Grace was intoned in Latin. Karen went to Commons if her gang, one of her gangs, was going as an alternative to a having sandwich in the buttery.

I ask her to describe what it feels like to be part of a privileged island community in the middle of a city that, at the time, was struggling economically. 'Oh,' briskly, 'physical location was not a factor.' Then, more thoughtfully, 'Well, maybe it was. It was an enclosed campus, a city within a city, a cocoon, that's for sure. You had your own social life in there. Of course you went out to discos and so on, but you went in a pack.'

And the privileged bit?

'Yes. Of course. Privileged to be there.'

That wasn't really the question. But two of the most attractive features of Karen Erwin's positive and open-hearted personality are her directness and honesty. A third is her firm view that everyone, but everyone, deserves equal treatment and respect. After a few seconds' thought, she amends her statement. 'Privileged to be there, yes, but really, you're right to ask. As students, nobody gave a thought to the outside and the underprivileged. Well, not many.'

So what about the inspiration behind Human Need

Week, then? Was that not run as a counterfoil to the 'privileged' tag that in the past was habitually hung round the neck of the feckless creature known, probably since the days of J. P. Donleavy and his *Ginger Man*, as 'the Trinity Student'? Was it a guilt thing? Even a teeny one?

'Ah, no. There was no communal altruism. Most of the people who were on the altruistic committees were on them just for the organisational buzz. The altruism was vague.'

From as early as 1873 the college, fiercely determined to maintain independence at all costs, repelled efforts to encourage or even force it to amalgamate with other educational establishments. Or, at least, become more visibly and actually inclusive. But it was during Karen's time, while independence was still paramount, that the authorities realised Trinity could no longer isolate itself from an inexorably changing world.

'There was a quiet revolution going on in Trinity. It had been West Brit and Protestant Ascendancy and so forth, and there was still a bit of that in places like the Boat Club, but Catholics, both British and Irish, were beginning to arrive, as were people from the North of Ireland.

'What's more, it wasn't just the Beat the Ban Catholics coming in specifically to make a point. The energy had gone out of that, and they were now trickling in without asking for permission. Archbishop McQuaid's sway had lessened. All that unrest was over.' During his reign, the Archbishop of Dublin had forbidden Catholics in his diocese to cross Trinity's apostate threshold and granted 'dispensations' to very few.

Although the college had accepted applications from Roman Catholics since 1793, not many took up the offer, so it instituted 'non-foundation' all-denomination scholarships in 1854, and by 1873 had abolished all religious tests for entry, except those connected with its Divinity School. Karen McDowell's contemporaries, living fast and immersed in their own affairs, rarely stopped to analyse any of this, but looking back, she does remember the consciousness, within Trinity's old walls, of being part of 'a liberal minority with freedom of thought'.

To get back to those walls, that hallowed physical environment, there must have been some feeling of antiquity, of history?

'Physically, I agree, it was a magical place.' She spent a lot of time mooching across and around Front Square, 'where part of the entertainment was to watch tourists surreptitiously kicking at ancient cobblestones in an attempt to loosen one, pocket it and take it back to Boise'.

As a body, did students resent the tourists' intrusion on their turf?

'Not personally, I don't think. We knew that to Trinity, they were dollars on feet.' But she admits that a cohort did snigger at the Crimplened unfortunates who asked for directions to 'Kelly's Book'; also those who, in response to, 'Where's the Book of Kells?' loved to snap back: 'In Kells!'

She was so active, and with a finger in so many pies, during those four years that 'to this day, someone will appear on TV and – it has become a catch-cry in our house – I'll pop up and I'll say to the boys, "He was in college with me! Or, Oh, look, she was in college with me . . ." She lists a few of the college's movers and shakers who were among her contemporaries, easily identifiable even then as future influencers: Michael Colgan, Dick Spring, Paul McGuinness, Mary Harney, the current director of public prosecutions, James Hamilton . . .

Apart from the liberal education and the closeted nursery time available to discover where your real talents may lie in an extraordinary and very beautiful environment, the advantage of a Trinity education, of hobnobbing with movers and shakers, persists. Karen still knows everyone.

'But it's not only Trinity. It's the same for everyone in Dublin, really. In Dublin, you always know someone, or know of someone, who will know someone else.'

Aidan Mathews's Aristotelian polity again, then.

The Seven – or Nine – Churches

I cannot resist this story. Although it has nothing whatsoever to do with Dublin, it has everything to do with the kind of blood that runs in the veins of Miss Kelly, who very definitely is a Dubliner. Her name is Anne, but even after years in the employ of the jeweller for whom she works as a bookkeeper – and whom she has led on innumerable tours of her beloved Italy – her boss would never refer to her as anything but 'Miss Kelly'.

To set the scene: we are in the sitting room of Miss Kelly's house. The room is small, and although there is a television set, the shelves and surfaces are crammed mostly with souvenirs, records and books. There are books and magazines in the hallway too. Miss Kelly reads a lot: 'Biographies, history and so forth'. She is tiny, with bright, shrewd eyes, and though she is not young, her laugh is that of a girl.

We are here because she is to help me with identification of the Seven Churches (or 'Seven Chapels' as that Protestant, Les Coleman, would have it). As we know, priests, friends' aunts, Aidan Mathews and books on Old Dublin were aware of the Holy Thursday ritual, but I remained in the dark as to *which* seven were those ordained. Miss Kelly would know, I was told by my brother, Declan, an authority on most things, whose steer in this case proved, once again, reliable. Yet before I reveal what she told me, I simply must relay the story of Miss Kelly's deceased grand-aunt.

First you have to know that Miss Kelly's maternal forebears, a landed Carlow family named Oliver, were comfortably off. There were three Oliver sisters, Miss Kelly's grandmother, Anne, an Elizabeth 'who married the paymaster general in New York', and a sister who became Sister Mary Francis when she went into a convent in Skibbereen to finish her education and never came out. They got her fortune! At that time the fortune [dowry] was kept – invested – on the off chance that the nun would have to leave.' Miss Kelly's sister did stay, however, and throughout her life, 'sent us the most delightful letters and little *Agnus Deis* and scapulars. And we'd send her a box of sweets.'

About eight years ago, in 1999, when Miss Kelly and her sister were on holiday not far from Skibbereen, they decided to visit their grand-aunt's grave. They found it easily enough in the nuns' cemetery in the grounds of the convent in question, 'and when we were looking at it a nun came up to us: "Can I help you?"'

They explained who they were. The nun was delighted to meet them and insisted that they come in. 'We have one nun left who'd remember Sister Mary Francis. She was a very brave lady.'

She sure was.

'A vessel pulled into Cobh. The captain sent word that he had a man on board suffering from smallpox and wanted to get the man to a hospital. The crew were terrified to have anything to do with him and he was literally dying from lack of attention.'

In Cobh, however, they demurred a bit. 'They said they had no facilities. But someone said, "Try the convent. There are nursing sisters there."

'So they tried the convent and the reverend mother asked the nuns if any of them would volunteer. My grand-aunt said she would go, and another nun said she'd join her. So they were tendered out to the ship, went on board and the two of them nursed the man to health.'

With commendable understatement, Miss Kelly adds that Sister Mary Francis contracted 'a touch of the disease' in a hand and arm. 'She lost slight use of her left hand. She didn't mind. She just took it. They were so religious. The shipping-line owners in gratitude and appreciation sent a donation to the convent.'

Miss Kelly cannot put her finger on precisely the date at which these events occurred, but estimates it would have been in the late 1880s.

Miss Kelly, you see, who keeps meticulous accounts for her employer and who is forever planning their next trip to Italy together, is ninety years old.

Her grandfather, who came from farming stock in a place where he and his brothers were also required by their father to serve their time at smithing – 'to take their turn at the family forge' – came to Dublin to work as a steelsmith in the Inchicore Railway Works. As part of his employment conditions, he was granted a company house. 'My mother was born in that house, I was born in that house. But, of course, we were all fired out when I was seven. The house died with my grandfather.'

For the next few years, the Kellys moved from flat to corporation house and back to flat again, all in the environs of Inchicore. 'Our lives were bounded by the Works. The horn went off at a quarter to one and the dinner was on the table at one o'clock when my father came in. Nothing was wasted. My mother never believed in peeling potatoes. They were cooked in their skins, peeled on the dish and the peelings put in a bucket for the pig man when he came around with his slops cart. Those potatoes were snowy white and the cabbage was fantastic. We always had our own cabbage. My father, a countryman at heart, grew it in the plots, what they call allotments now.' The one reserved to the Kellys was among 'a swathe on the way down to where the Memorial Garden is now'.

Despite his inherited smithing skills, Miss Kelly's father decided to open a grocer's shop in Inchicore, with patchy success initially. The first attempt was lost 'over a bad debt', the second looked promising, but then a partner pulled out before it had even got off the ground. He persisted, though, 'and when we were young children we grew up in a grocer's shop. We learned to be mannerly to the customers, to say, "Yes, ma'am" and "Thank you, sir."'

Their home enjoyed gaslight, but no gas cookers. However, her father called on the family skills and fashioned an iron bracket under the gas wall-lamp, diverting the gas supply to it 'so that in the mornings he was able to boil water in an enamel kettle, enough for a cup of tea'. There were hazards with this arrangement. When an overnight guest was staying in the parlour downstairs, Miss Kelly's mother, in bed above, smelled gas and went down to investigate. On retiring for the night, the guest, from the country and used to paraffin lamps, had blown out the flame on the gas.

Recreation for the two Kelly girls was simple. Their father took them with him when he went fishing on the Liffey and 'we'd play on the banks. We'd make little houses for ourselves from the blackberry plants and the leaves and so on, but my father was always warning us, "Be careful where you put them because there's an otter around here and he won't be too happy if you're in his way!"'

They went for walks along what they referred to as the Liffey Walk, from Inchicore, through Islandbridge and all the way to Palmerstown. Moreover, if they were thirsty, they could stop to drink at a 'beautiful natural spring'.

If the rhythm of their lives was bounded by the Works, the Church was at the centre of it. Novenas, devotions, processions, the Forty Hours' Adoration, preparations for Communion and Confirmation, sodality, retreats. 'We even had the Children's Retreat.'

When the time came for employment, Miss Kelly's sister became a teacher in Goldenbridge Convent school for a while, then married.

Miss Kelly took a job in a grocery on the South Circular Road, 'from nine-thirty a.m. to nine p.m. I hated every minute of it. I had all the rough work to do, lifting fifty-pound blocks of butter, sterilising, scrubbing the floor white in the morning, scrubbing the counters.' She was give one half-day off per week. The half-day started at four o'clock.

What was more, she was working without pay. 'This was "training".'

The shop was in the Jewish quarter 'but we got no special orders. They had their own shops for their unleavened bread and their oils. We sold a lot of dripping and lard.' There was one Orthodox lady, 'all dressed in black with a black ribbon around her neck and hair severely pulled back', who, on the Sabbath, used to call on Miss Kelly to light the gas on the cooker for her. And, as she was only a trainee shop assistant, lady customers ignored her when they were discussing their skivvies: 'I'm not entirely satisfied with her but she does make the beds nicely.'

One poor girl used to come into Miss Kelly's shop with the list of messages 'and she'd nearly fall asleep on the counter while she was waiting for the order to be filled'. Miss Kelly, just a girl herself, became very concerned: '"You're very tired?"

'"Can't get a wink of sleep with that shower."

'The housemaid's bed was on the settle in the kitchen and most nights the sons of the house and their cronies played cards in that kitchen until the early hours of the morning and she had to wait until they were finished before she could go to bed.'

Miss Kelly's uncle, with whom she used to spend summer holidays in the country, was a tailor: 'He would always make me a lovely coat for coming back to Dublin.' During one such holiday, Miss Kelly decided she might give up the grocery business and apprentice herself to a dressmaker. She found a position in a 'couture' fashion house, Cecile, on Baggot Street, near Fitzwilliam Square, where she enjoyed (a debatable) special status: 'I was to work for the first three months for nothing. But that was a concession. You usually had to pay a fee.'

Within days, she knew she wouldn't make it in that business either. 'I'd never have the nerve to do what she did. She would take a piece of material and drape it over the form and, without a pattern, cut strategically into it.'

There were no tea breaks and dinner was strictly from one until two when Miss Kelly usually went walking in Fitzwilliam Square to clear her head. Most of her days were spent collecting fabric ('She always said I had an eye for the different shades of black') delivering finished garments or, in the workroom, oversewing the raw edges of inside hems. She detested the tedium of this, especially when tennis frocks became all the rage and the belts were stiffened by being sewn with 'rows and rows and rows of contrasting thread in navy or dark blue'.

The last straw came during a bus strike.

By then she was living on the North Circular Road at

Prussia Street and, during the strike, had to walk to Baggot Street every morning and home again in the evenings. She was getting progressively more fatigued, but kept going.

Then, one day, on a Saturday, which was supposed to be her half-day, the proprietor promised a good customer that 'my little girl' would deliver a tennis frock that afternoon for a tournament in the evening. The customer lived in Dartry, on the far side of Rathmines.

'Remember, I had already walked in from the North Circular Road and here I had to walk all the way to Dartry from Baggot Street and back home to the North Circular Road from there.' The only way she could make it home without dropping was carefully to plan her homeward route so that it passed a series of churches where, every so often, she could stop for a few minutes' rest in a pew. Nevertheless she arrived home in a state of almost total collapse.

What nobody knew at the time, least of all herself, was that the underlying cause of her extreme fatigue, understandable on the surface, especially on that Saturday, was as a result of pernicious anaemia. On medical advice, she left that job. She would have left it anyhow.

She went on to Commercial College, found she had a 'great head for figures' and answered an advertisement for 'a girl to write up accounts' with Comerford and Brady, specialist engravers and metalworkers in Fleet Street 'where the ESB is now'. The firm worked and engraved all metals, brass, silver, gold and even steel: 'We did all the big brass plates for Dame Street.' In those days Dame Street was lined with finance offices and other 'professional' premises.

She waxes lyrical about the quality of the workmanship with which she was surrounded. Mr Comerford himself 'told stories about his childhood and being a chorister in St Patrick's Cathedral' while he did magnificent work, 'especially on church patens.' High praise from someone, who, because of her own family speciality, knew her metalwork.

For the next twenty-eight years, Miss Kelly worked there with 'very nice people', and was happy. There was one hiccup, however, which clouds the sunny atmosphere in her little sitting room.

A friend of a friend of a relative left in a pair of earrings for refurbishment – the work was being done as a favour – and implied that when she had collected them she had in fact gone home empty-handed. Miss Kelly knew that she had handed them over. The customer was insistent: the earrings were now missing.

Well, that customer didn't know who she was dealing with, did she? After a sleepless night spent casting this way and that, examining her own actions – could she have made a mistake; could the customer be right, she had been most insistent – Miss Kelly telephoned the woman first thing the following morning. '"Did you find the earrings"?'

'"Oh," carelessly, "Yes I did."

'"That's fine. But it would have been nice if you'd told us."

'She found her earrings,' Miss Kelly marched straight up to Mr Comerford. 'But she didn't have the manners to let us know. To ease my mind.'

The lady in question never got that type of favour again. Neither did any other friends-of-friends. End of special favours at Comerford and Brady.

Miss Kelly has eased back to part-time work now for her current employer, who had come in to Comerford and Brady as an apprentice: 'There were two gentlemanly boys and he was one of them.' Now she merely keeps his books for him and plans their trips to Italy because he is interested in what she is interested in: 'Travel and stories and gardening, nice things to look at, antiques and that kind of thing.' (And in case I am inclined to forget my Aristotelian polity, this employer was also brought up in Cameron Square, home of Les Coleman . . .)

I almost forgot what I came for. What about the old Dublin ritual of the Seven Churches on Holy Thursday?

'It wasn't only religious, you know. It was sort of an outing. And there was a competitive element: we went around comparing altars and flowers and so on – that altar was good, those flowers were only so-so . . . No formal prayers. We genuflected and spent a few minutes adoring the Blessed Sacrament.'

Yes, but *which* churches are we talking about here?

The answer, if thorough, is a bit deflating, really. Turns out that Les Coleman, following the ritual with his Catholic pals, wasn't really cheating by visiting St Michael's in Inchicore more than once. 'It depended on where you lived. If you were in the country how would you get around unless you were lucky enough to have a donkey or a pony and trap?'

So it's not a ritual exclusive to, or even originating in, Dublin's inner core?

No.

Even more upsetting, though, is that in Dublin there are *no designated churches*. Like Les and his mates some years later, Miss Kelly and her pals always started at St Michael's – the Oblates in Inchicore. 'And then we'd work our way down to the Quays and across to the Capuchins in Church Street, then to Arran Quay and then we crossed the bridge back to the Franciscans, Adam and Eve's on Merchants Quay, and then to Michael and John's, and then we worked our way up the hill into High Street and St Audoen's, and then St Nicholas of Myra in Francis Street and St Catherine's in Meath Street and the Augustinians in Thomas Street, that was John's Lane. We did nine.'

There is a 'gotcha' glint in those bright eyes.

People Power

Miss Kelly's church in Inchicore has an interesting history. The present church succeeds one made of wood.

In the mid-nineteenth century, the Oblate order bought the site, but that was as far as it went. They were stuck for money, but also for ideas as to how to get it built.

Apparently, one young carpenter, hearing of their dilemma, came forward with a plan: if the good priests bought the timber, the nails and the glass, he would guarantee to have a church built within a week.

Supplies were bought and delivered to the site on Tuesday, 24 June 1856. That evening, seven hundred men, including the young carpenter, turned up and set to work. Each evening, after their paid work, they arrived to continue. And by the late evening of Saturday that week, they had finished, having built not only the church but the altar. It seated a thousand worshippers.

St Blaise and the Fourteen Holy Helpers

For Dubliners, as elsewhere in Ireland, the incidental church rituals came with a festive feel, especially in summer: Corpus Christi processions, for instance, May devotions . . .

Bernard Farrell mentioned the ritual attached to the feast day of St Blaise. Peter Sheridan did, too, although I did not include it in his interview. As the patron saint of throats, Blaise is important to actors and theatre people generally, although 'ordinary' Dubliners venerate him on his day.

Who was he, though?

He was an Armenian Christian bishop who in AD 316 was martyred for his faith. He was beheaded, but not before his living flesh was shredded with the long, needle-like tines of metal carding combs, used in spinning wool. His work with throats began when, on being conveyed to prison, he encountered a child who was choking on a fishbone and successfully interceded with God on the child's behalf.

In learning about him, I discovered he was part of a group previously unknown to me, the 'Fourteen Holy Helpers', each member particularly efficacious in the curing of specific illnesses in different parts of the body, and devotion to whom began in Germany during the Black Plague of 1348–1350. Each has a feast day in his or her own right, but as a group they were commemorated on 8 August until 1969, when in reforming the saints' calendar, the Pope abolished it as an officially sanctioned practice.

Opera buffs would know of the group because in Humperdinck's opera, *Hansel and Gretel,* one of the most beautiful – and moving – arias is a duet between two lost children who sing a night prayer:

> When at night I go to sleep,
> Fourteen angels watch to keep,
> Two my head are guarding,
> Two my feet are guiding,
> Two upon my right hand,
> Two upon my left hand,
> Two who warmly cover,
> Two who o'er me hover,
> Two to whom 'tis given,
> To guide my steps to Heaven.

Every year on Blaise's feast day, 3 February, when I was with the Abbey Theatre I remember Father Brian D'Arcy coming into the Queens with his two candles. He would never impose his presence – he was much too theatre-savvy for that – but would wait quietly until those actors who wished to have their throats blessed approached him, necks elongated.

Then he would touch each of us with the crossed candles and utter a blessing.

Some knelt. I didn't. I was young.

Father D'Arcy didn't react. He was used to people like me.

Always Trust St Jude

Ifaka Iaka hadaka gunaka Iaka wouldaka shootaka yonaka swanaka onaka ponaka.

Recognise that?

No, nothing to do with Armenian Holy Helpers, it was a doggerel that, as children, we chanted gaily for no reason whatsoever. Take away the 'aka' at the end of each word and what you're left with is: 'If I had a gun I would shoot yon swan on [the] pon[d].' Yeah. Bizarre.

For years, Liam Hayden and Geraldine Kelly used a similar but far more sophisticated method of communication on the floor of Frawleys of Thomas Street when there was something they didn't want a customer to understand. According to them, it is used widely in the retail trade.

Wemeratch hemer shemere permicks. Any guesses?

The code involves the addition of a syllable, mostly 'mer', to plain vanilla English. If it has to be inserted immediately after a consonant, a vowel is added. The above would be a response to spotting a lady with light fingers: 'Watch her. She picks!'

Geraldine is petite, elegant and looks twenty years

younger than her long service with the shop would indicate. He is stylish, too, animated like his colleague, solidly built and with bright, miss-nothing eyes. Of the two, he is the more talkative. On first meeting in the lobby at the Gresham, both give yours truly a lightning-fast once-over and yours truly feels she's failed the test. They don't mean to be impolite: from years of training in the clothing trade, the scan was automatic.

Both have the type of outgoing personality that makes for pleasurable company; both are inconsolable at Frawleys closure. Between them, they have given more than seventy years' service to the people of Thomas Street and throughout this interview, a refrain – 'it was a heartbreaker; it was heartbreaking' – leaks from both about the shop's demise.

As with Les Coleman, both started their retail careers with kicks up the transom from family. As soon as she reached fourteen, the legal age for leaving school, Geraldine did not even wait for the end of the school year. 'It was February. I wouldn't go back.'

Time passed and then her granny, who ran a grocery in Inchicore, stepped in. 'You needn't think you can be sitting around here . . . ' She tapped into her network. '"I'm going to ask Jim Bannon to ask Jim Lee to get you into Frawleys." So off I trotted next day on the bus and I'm thinking,' she pulls an expression filled with teenage disdain, '*Frawleys*? I'm not going to work in *Frawleys*!'

She goes into the shop. '"Hello, I'm Geraldine Kelly. Jim Bannon sent me. I'm fifteen in February."'

'"OK, start on Monday," said Jim Lee, proprietor, and turned away. That was the interview. I wasn't even brought up to the office.'

Liam was brought up to the office and it took him a little longer to get in. 'I left school at fifteen – I hated school. I got my Group Cert at James's Street Tech in 1963. They were building houses in Inchicore, I remember. I was sitting there on the wall one day, watching them build the houses, and my mother let a roar at me, "If you think you're going to sit there all day and watch them working you have another think coming. Go out and get yourself a job."'

His family's turn to tap into the network. They knew a retired gárda: 'Jim Ryan, God rest him, who used to walk the floor in Frawleys as security.' They contacted Jim and heard back that, yes, a young lad was wanted for Frawleys. In the stores.

'I went down for the interview and met the right honourable James Lee, who always looked extremely cross. So he says, "Come up to the office." Woodwormy chairs – and if you saw the *size* of it! They turned it into a toilet for the manager afterwards. And there were all these old photographs, old Con Frawley on a horse and cart . . .' Con and Bridget Frawley, from Limerick originally, founded the shop in 1892. They had no children and when they died their nephews, Jimmy and Jack, inherited the business.

On the day of his interview, Jim Lee gave Liam a pencil and 'this oul' brown paper bag. I can still see it, with "Frawleys" written on it in blue writing. "Add up this," he says.'

'The altar that Da built . . '
crowds of people watch the
Benediction Service,
O'Connell Street and Bridge,
Eucharistic Congress,
June 1932.

Container cargo, 1964-style

Christchurch Cathedral, 1950.

Corpus Christi procession,
Manor Street area, 1969.

Ogling an Aer Lingus Viscount
from the open-air viewing gallery
at Dublin Airport, 1962.

Another sale at Clerys, 1940s.

"They're GORGEOUS!" Rolling Stones concert, Adelphi, 1966.

'A little straw hat with the streaming blue ribbons is soon to come dancing over the bridge.'–James Thomson: 'Sunday Up the River'. At the Iveagh Markets, 1950s.

To market via the North Circular Road, at Phibsboro, St Peter's church in the background.

*Dublin Castle,
including the
medieval Record
Tower. Illustration
by Pat Liddy.*

*Walking the wall above
Sandymount Strand, 1969.*

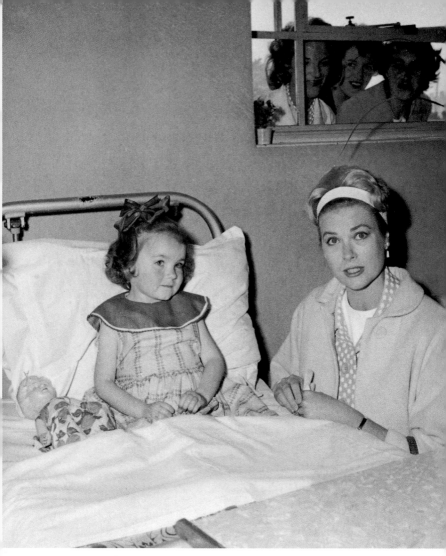

Princess Grace of
Monaco, visiting
Our Lady's Children's
Hospital, Crumlin,
June, 1961.

'"2/lld

'"4/11d

'"9/11d

'"1/1d – "'

Young Hayden added it up. He got it right. That was the interview. Jim Lee dismissed him. 'Start on Monday.'

But there was a sting in the tail.

'I was walking out the door and I had a lovely suit on. I can still see the suit, two buttons on the back and a half-belt, the only suit I ever possessed.' The suit didn't cut the mustard with Jim Lee, though. "don't wear that when you're coming in," he called after me. "I don't like it."

Young Hayden got the hump on. 'I was disgusted.' So disgusted he didn't turn up on the Monday. Instead, he went to work for Nicholson Brothers, wholesalers to the retail clothing trade in South William Street, and spent the next five years there. He was happy. 'Romper suits, I can still see them, and Belinda baby pants, but at the back of my mind I knew I always wanted to work in a shop. Maybe it was in the family. My grandmother had a shop years ago and all of my father's side were in some kind of shop business down in Carlow or some place like that. Hucksters' shops.'

Jimmy and Jack Lee were customers of Nicholsons: 'Jimmy didn't remember me, of course, but I used to be doing up the orders for them and I was always asking about vacancies but there was never a vacancy, never. People came to work in Frawleys and they stayed for decades. It was a great family and friendship place.' He becomes a little emotional and looks into the distance. 'I really, really miss it . . .

'Anyway, I used to be doing the novena to St Jude. Up in Whitefriar Street every Tuesday night. To get a job. My father had died and my mother was unwell. She was doing the novena to St Jude for me as well.'

Next thing his mother was coming round the corner of Meath Street when she bumped into Paddy O'Dea from County Clare, who worked in Frawleys: 'How'ya, ma'am?' They recognised each other.

'"I've a young lad at home," she goes, "any chance of a job in Frawleys for him? I'm doing the novena to St Jude and he is too."'

Always trust St Jude. 'Send him in to me, ma'am, send him in,' said Paddy O'Dea. 'I've a young lad leaving.'

Nearly six years older and a good deal wiser, Liam went back up to the same office and had a *déjà-vu* interview: 'The same brown bag with the blue writing, the same sums.' He got it right again, and was not wearing the suit, so he was in. That was November 1968 and he stayed until retirement. 'To tell you truthfully, it broke my heart the day I walked out of it.'

They agree that, underneath the gruff exterior, Jimmy Lee was 'the kindest man under the sun'. Geraldine, though, has an addendum: 'He'd roar at you from one end of the store to the other if a customer was looking for something and you'd sent him to the wrong place. The whole thing was the customer, the customer, the customer.'

The goods – bloomers, shop coats, crossover aprons – arrived in bales, wrapped in brown paper and tied with twine. They were put up on the shelves in the same state. In her early days there, Geraldine was fascinated by an unusual skill displayed by the men: 'The way they'd reach up behind them and flip down the parcels of goods from the shelves, the way they'd break the string with just their hands.'

Break string with their hands?

Liam tries to demonstrate. It involves looping the twine round the palm of one hand, hooking it on to a little finger, then chucking hard: 'You got very used to it. It got easy, except for that big, hairy twine.'

Don't try this at home. 'If you didn't know how to do it, you'd take the finger off yourself.'

Parcels and parcelling were a huge component of the job. 'Someone would ask for an overall.' This is Geraldine. 'You'd have to open the parcel, take one out, and she'd hold it up to her and mightn't even buy it – and then you'd have to fold it up, put it back in the parcel, wrap it up again and tie it.' Rolls of both paper and twine, for wrapping eventual purchases, were kept on every countertop.

Meanwhile, the floor would be piled high with parcels of all shapes and sizes, securely tied and labelled. Liam explains the system. A man would choose a duffel coat or a suit – these arrived in bundles within huge skips – and would pay a deposit for it. His garment was wrapped and tied with a docket that would show how much was paid, how much owed. He, or most likely his wife, would come in weekly from then on to pay a bit off until the great day when he or she could collect the parcel. 'So you had to be able to make neat parcels.'

Those Frawleys customers were 'the salt of the earth'. Liam and Geraldine trip over each other to acknowledge this. 'They loved us. Mind you,' they look at each other, 'if they didn't like you, you might as well leave the area!'

Liam: 'You always felt safe with them. Bridgefoot Street wasn't a nice street years ago, you wouldn't want to walk down there but if you did and you got any hassle from someone, all the others'd muck in: "Leave him alone. He's from Frawleys." You'd probably dressed them since the time they were children.' Bridgefoot Street, by the way, was where the poor and homeless congregated at the Hot Wall. This was an exposed wall of Thompson's bakery, on the other side of which were the ovens, radiating heat to the needy.

'You mightn't know everyone you served, but everyone you served knew you. I was digging my garden yesterday and a binman comes up the road – never saw him before in my life, as far as I know.' This binman stopped to survey the digging. 'First time I ever saw you do a bit of work. You didn't work as hard as that when you were in Frawleys!'

After the final closure, Geraldine sought work elsewhere. The day before this interview, she had started in Guineys of North Earl Street and a couple of hours before she came up to talk to me, she was putting up a sale poster in the display window when she got a tap on the shoulder from a woman: 'I'm delighted. Great to see you down here. You weren't owa of a job long!' And while Liam was waiting for her outside the shop, 'This oul' one comes up to me, holding up something. "What d'ya think of that? Would that look well? How much is that?"

'"Sorry, love, I'm not part of the staff here." She stands back, considering. "I know you from somewhere," and goes off, shaking her head.'

Geraldine: 'They mixed up Frawleys and Guineys. They'd be looking for something and we wouldn't have it and they'd nod: "Don't worry, love. I'll get it in your other branch."

'"But we don't have another branch."

'"Ah you do, love. You know the one in North Earl Street, or is it Talbot Street?"'

At this point it might be worth pointing out that although Michael Guiney of the North Earl Street shop is a nephew of the late Denis Guiney of Clerys, with branches in Talbot Street, the original Guineys, founded (and burned down in 1921, then resurrected) by Denis Guiney himself in Talbot Street prior to his takeover of Clerys, is actually an offshoot of the bigger store. Guineys and Michael Guineys are related but different.

That clear?

Like Guineys, Frawleys embodied the pile-em-high-sell-em-cheap philosophy. Goods were sold directly out of the parcels and cardboard boxes, and when they were hung on display, the aisles were so overcrowded they were virtually invisible. Geraldine 'cringed in the old days if I saw someone coming in in a wheelchair'. But the formula was so successful that on a Saturday afternoon the floor was so jammed with shoppers that the assistants could not move from one side of the shop to the other. If they needed change, for instance, they had to yell and wave pound notes in the air, hoping to attract attention from someone, anyone.

Recycling (or parsimony) was *de rigueur*. 'We never bought a display ticket in our lives.' Instead staff were under orders to retain sheets of cardboard stiffening enclosed in kids' anoraks. 'We'd have to cut them up to make tickets for display.'

Liam explains that Frawleys' success was due not just to the cheapness of its stock. 'We prided ourselves on personal service.' He bemoans the lack of it nowadays. In the men's department of a Dublin branch of a large UK chain just days before this interview, he had seen a 'foreign' man ask an assistant if there was any shirt cheaper than the one he was holding, only to get the offhand response: '"That's all we have." I wanted to go across to the salesperson and say, "Look, I'll give you an hour and show you how to do it. I'll even teach you for nothing!"'

In fact he did 'walk around a bit', trying to decide if he would actually do this, when 'out of the corner of my eye I saw I was being followed by a plain-clothes security guy'.

He left.

Geraldine chimes in: 'You *never* say, "It's over there." You *never* point.'

Liam explains how personal service works.

Their shop specialised in outsize menswear and 'made a

fortune out of it, men up to sixty waist and twenty-four collar. Every customer would spend at least two to three hundred euro with you because they couldn't get the clothes or the service anywhere else.'

A man might be going to the checkout, 'maybe with underwear 4XL. Now if this was Dunnes' checkout they'd just take the money off you, twenty-three or thirty euro and you're stuck with that because you can't change underwear. But if it was me, I would go up to him and I'd say, "Do you mind my saying to you – is that for yourself or for somebody else?" 'And he'd say, "That's for myself." 'I'd get him the right size. And he wouldn't be insulted.'

Frawleys sold not only clothes but furniture, bedding, household goods, toys. (Geraldine's first assignment was to sell Crolly Dolls in the toy department.) 'They used to come into the curtain department.' Liam does a fair imitation of an oul' wan. "I want curtains for me front window."

'"OK, ma'am. What's the measurement?"

'"Oh, well, I don't know, but they're the houses up in Crumlin. You know the houses up there, don't you?"'

Or: '"I want a bit of lino for me floor."

'"What size are you looking for, ma'am?"

'And she takes out a piece of twine with knots in it: "Now me cooker's from here to here," showing the distance between two of the knots, "and here's me sink . . ." That woman got her lino. And it fitted exactly. That was the service you got in Frawleys.'

As in Bests, commission was everything. Each staff

member was assigned a letter, which they punched in when putting money into the till. Competition was fierce, with some arguing that making eye-contact with a customer was a legitimate claim to ownership of that person.

Both crease on remembering the story of the two staff who were carrying a wardrobe up the stairs to the furniture department, one bent double with the piece on his back, the second steadying and pushing from below. Apparently it was being paid for on the drip and when they were half-way up the stairs with it, the guy who was behind, pushing, spotted its potential owner on the shop floor asking plaintively for service. 'I want to pay a bit off of me wardrobe.' He left the beast of burden to it (which almost poleaxed him) and raced down to take the customer's part-payment, tilling it with his letter, which would guarantee his commission.

There were consequences, of course: 'The two of them asked each other out the back for a fight. Would you believe it? Middle-aged men! Both of them nearly pensioners!' Liam has to wipe away tears of laughter.

He wrote a poem for Frawleys' centenary celebrations and was as proud as punch when the management put it in the window.

> In years to come our minds will wander,
> We'll think of days that used to be,
> Of times we spent in dear old Frawleys,
> The value centre of the Liberties . . .
> John's Lane bells ring out so gaily,
> Our hearts will echo with their chimes,

For we are proud that we have been
With Dublin in the rare old times.

That last stanza turns out to have been prophetic because on 2 June 2007, the day Frawleys finally closed its doors, pride in what they and their company had achieved for the community kept the staff going, although it was diluted with real tears, theirs and those of their customers – 'The number of elderly people who were in, crying, that day . . .'

They received Mass cards, wine, chocolates and other gifts, even money. Liam speaks softly of the old lady who struggled all the way up from the end of Meath Street. 'The poor lady was barely able to walk. She was crying, "I'm going to miss you terrible, thanks for everything."' Liam had dressed the woman's disabled son. He had died at twenty-one.

That evening at home, Liam opened some of the cards and envelopes the customers had pressed into his hand that day. 'A fifty-euro note . . . And one of them had a beautiful watch attached . . .' The woman who had given it to him had put her phone number on the card. He rang to thank her. '"You shouldn't have done that, ma'am." And she said, "You were very good to me over the years."'

For that woman and countless others, Frawleys was more than a shop for the Thomas Street area: it was a social service. 'It was like hearing confessions.' They heard people's most intimate problems, some of them physical but some, it has to be said, even comical. Here's Geraldine, heartfelt, about the shoe department: 'At least there'll be no more bunions!'

'Yeah,' says Liam. 'No more "I'm crucified with the bunion – can I show it to you?"'

However, a great many of the problems the customers brought to Frawleys were far from comical for the people concerned. Mothers with fat children came to Frawleys because they couldn't get anything to fit them elsewhere. 'And we'd measure them and get the clothes made up for them in our suppliers.' There was no premium put on this bespoke service. 'We put only the usual mark-up on them, the same you'd have on any of the clothes.'

Liam had another customer who came regularly to him 'with a son who had a very bad kidney problem, very bloated and so on. And like that, we used to get the trousers made up for him. From the time he was a little fella of about four, up to the time he was about twelve.

'We treated them with dignity. The day Frawleys closed, we lost part of old Dublin. They'll make it into clubs and pubs and there won't be room for people like us any more.'

More's the pity.

And here, definitively, is why. 'Another lady came in to me with a card when we were closing. I wouldn't know her if she walked in the door right now. She came over to me. "I'm very sorry you're closing. Can I say something to you? Thanks for looking after us when we had nothing. You don't know me, but I pray for you every day of my life and I didn't even know your name until lately."

'"Pray for me? Do you? Why?"

'"You don't remember me. I brought in my little boy in a wheelchair many, many years ago to be dressed for his First Holy Communion. You lifted him out of the wheelchair and put him sitting on the counter and you treated him as if he was gold. I've never forgotten you for it."'

The Bells! The Bells!
The Sweet and Stinking Smells!

Bong! Bingitty Bingitty Bing Bong Bing! During her
childhood and young adulthood when Catherine Hogan
woke up on Sunday mornings just yards from Frawleys, she
might have thought she had been transported to Rome, such
was the tintinabulation of bell-ringing in the Thomas Street
air. Living within the Powers Distillery complex beside the
Clock pub and at the top of Meath Street, she and her family
were regularly entertained, or deafened, by the voices of the
churches around her, including the authoritative cathedral
boom of Saint Patrick's and Christchurch.

It wasn't only on Sunday mornings: 'I associate the bells
with trying to finish my last bit of homework for Monday
and these bells would be bonging and clanging. Bell-ringing
practice.'

Mind you, the Roman illusion was transient, because
although it did not operate on Sundays, olfactory traces of
the slaughterhouse just off Meath Street, near where the
Vicar Street entertainment venue is now, were permanently
in the air. 'I saw the animals down there. I knew they were

frightened. One got out, it may have been a little calf, but that was an area we never asked about – don't go there, don't ask about that . . .'

Catherine is blessed with one of the most naturally beautiful voices in Irish broadcasting. A trained and very talented musician, she and her co-host, Barry McGovern, won a Jacobs Award for the children's radio programme *Knock on the Door* but you can Google her to your heart's content, even trawl the RTÉ website, and you won't find any trace of her presence at the station. She is one of thos foundation people, an announcer, virtually anonymous, without whom Radio One could not function half as it does.

Her father, John Hogan, was chief distiller and dist manager at Powers, a major employer in Dublin of lorry drivers, mechanics, engineers, skilled labourers and professionals from many disciplines, including a chemist. Founded in 1791 (and the inventor of the miniature bottle, the 'Baby Power' in which my generation of girls took their milk to school), its internal streets retained their cobbles, laid originally to give purchase to the factory's horses. In Catherine's time it offered a 'fabulous restaurant' to its executives and a first-class canteen for the general workers.

With no garden attached to the multi-storey house that came with the job, Catherine and her five siblings, Bosco, Declan, Laurence, Helen and Angela, had to carve out spaces and nooks for themselves within the factory. They roller-skated: 'There were mini-railways – two polished parallel pieces of wood for the barrels to be rolled down into the cellars. We used to skate down this because it was lovely and smooth and there was even a ski-jump, a sort of copper hump you could jump over. It was like skateboarding is today.'

Dodging boilers and laboratories, they played hide-and-seek in tunnels, warehouses, offices, storehouses, on gantries, staircases and overhead walkways. They also had to keep an eye out for the moving grain trucks and other rolling stock about the vast concourse.

She managed to play tennis there, and to sunbathe, hitting volleys between the pitched roofs on some of the roofs from which she customarily descended covered in coal smuts. The distillery sported huge chimney stacks so 'There was a pall of smoke and a permanent smell of soot even inside the house. You'd blow your nose and what came out in your handkerchief was black.' Although she took it for granted at the time, in thinking back she is almost overawed as she describes the tremendous heat from the boiler-houses and the mash tuns; to tend the latter, the workers wore a type of karate suit with wide-legged pants and a belted top, made of thick cotton to absorb the sweat.

In retrospect, all these images are fascinating, but at the time she 'envied my friends who had ordinary front and back gardens'. Her mother, too, longed for somewhere to hang out the washing, but had to manage with a pulley airer in the kitchen. Not on Fridays, though: 'If Mum was making chips on a Friday she could never do washing. You'd be stinking of fat for the week.'

Just as childhood Dublin was a city of smells for Peter Sheridan, Catherine's Dublin, her Thomas Street, was too. And it is not only the abattoir that remains: 'Some of the smells were lovely, especially around September when we were going back to school,' when the street was scented with the sweetish fragrance of barley. 'Our house was built over the Corn Arch, a big double gate facing down Meath Street. As the delivery lorries got bigger and bigger, they started taking lumps off the stone,' but the scent passed right under her bedroom window.

The hops being trundled into the Guinness Brewery down the street were part of this harvest mix: 'One was like coffee roasting, the other was the smell of the country.' The combination was gorgeous.

In any month, however, to walk up that street was to walk through an aromatic buffet, especially on Fridays, when fish was added to the displays on the street-traders' vegetable and fruit stalls. There was the medicinal smell from Mushatt's Chemists, whose proprietary cough bottle, it was said, would take barnacles off a ship but would cure anything; the wet-washing smell venting from the Swastika Laundry; the cornucopia of scents from the grocery known as the Blanchardstown Mills. 'They made their own flour. Stone-ground flour milled out the back. You went in and everything was faintly covered in white, even the beautiful mosaic floor, the wooden counters and the coats of the staff. And, of course, there was horse poo everywhere from the Guinness drays. Dad used to send out one of the men to collect it off the street. Great for the rhubarb.'

Rhubarb? They grew rhubarb?

I had heard right. They might not have had a proper garden, but within the distillery, the family had use of an acre of coarse grass, spread over the roofs of adjoining warehouses. 'They'd grown potatoes there, apparently, during the Second World War. My dad cultivated part of it for rhubarb and vegetables. He gathered manure and seaweed for it so he could stay in touch with the land.' Mr Hogan, originally from Co. Waterford, a big, bluff man, was never happier than when he was picking sloes from the hedgerows every autumn to make his private brand of Hogan's sloe gin. This was in addition to the day job when, during the busy autumn season, he was on call during the night, every night, doing his rounds a couple of times 'to see that everything was ticking over nicely, that the coal boilers were properly stoked up and so on'.

Getting up to John Hogan's personal and unusual eyrie was not easy and it is doubtful if today's protective parents would allow their children unsupervised access to it as Catherine's did. 'It was a sizeable distance from the house. It took about twenty minutes to get there.' She relives the climbing and clambering, gesturing as she travels. 'There was the house-ey bit, and you crossed by a bridge over Oliver Bond Street at the back of the distillery, then you wound your way through the distillery, through all this machinery and these huge chains, up, upwards all the time, until you went up these next narrow stairways and then up to a door, which opened out on to this coarse grass . . .' When you got there, there were no railings, walls or balustrades to protect you from falling off.

If the distillery was their playground, the Phoenix Park, not far away, was the Hogan family's real garden. 'Dad made it his own. He went there every day after work for walks.' *En famille*, they brought picnics and 'he would always find the spot that was the least frequented, maybe near the Castleknock Gate or somewhere like that.' They would bring their dog too. 'Dad would drive slowly along the Polo Grounds with the dog in hot pursuit.' It jumped over anyone lying in its path.

The Hogans' home was wreathed in incense each year on the Feast of Corpus Christi. The distillery stored – and maintained – the papal flag and large altar used for the open-air Mass, the centrepiece of the area's huge procession. The distillery workers flew the flag from a pole over the house and erected the altar in and around the Corn Arch, chosen because it faced Meath Street. This allowed the crowds to pack, cruciform-style, into three vantage-points, Meath Street itself, and then up and down Thomas Street.

The family was, oddly, of the street and simultaneously not of it. 'I felt like an outsider. A middle-class daughter of the Big House.' The feeling strengthened each time the group of old men who regularly gathered at the front door of the house to chew the fat 'would shuffle to one side and doff their hats when I, as a child, came out. Mum used to pass on Dad's shirts and shoes and suit jackets to them and they were absolutely delighted. It didn't feel like charity and they didn't take it as such.

'One of the fruit vendors at the stalls across the road used to think that Mum was Mrs Power. Her name was Mrs Thomas, such a lovely woman, a big round lady. We always had masses of fruit. She'd give Mum the stuff that was still all right but just about to go: "you have a big family, ma'am, God bless them."' The same stallholder gave wedding presents to each of the three 'Powers' girls when their time came: a satiny quilt, a gilded vase, a lamp.

The house had five bedrooms and five flights of stairs. Top to bottom, the curved banisters, sashed windows and ornamental brasses shone with the exertions of Catherine's mother and Mrs McCormack, the charlady, both of whom waged a ceaseless battle against the Curse of the Smuts. Mrs McCormack lived in a one-roomed flat in a tall tenement in High Street, no trace of which now remains. When the street was widened, the family was one of those rehomed by the Corporation to the acres of Crumlin. Mrs McCormack soon found the journey to Thomas Street beyond her capabilities so she sent her daughter to continue in her place.

Catherine and her friend Maria, from the Mayo Stores, bought their first bras together in Frawleys, and if the staff there considered their shop to be the major landmark on Thomas Street, as they certainly did, the Hogans reckoned there were three: their distillery, Guinness's and John's Lane church, just across from one of the distillery buildings; 'that church was huge in our lives.' It was not just the bell-ringing, it was Confession and Communion, priests available when necessary – and, of course, Mass. 'They had awful trouble with pigeons, inside and outside.' All during the services the officiating priest could hardly hear himself with the billing, cooing and fluttering high in the roof as the birds went about their business, some of it filthy. (Ask Kevin Hough about the doves that belonged to the Great Gambani!)

Churchgoers tolerated the missiles and the fluttering, especially at the twelve-fifteen Mass, because that was when Daniel McNulty, whose blindness was no handicap to the virtuosity of his organ-playing, accompanied the service and performed 'a little mini-recital' afterwards for which everyone stayed.

Like North Earl Street in Frank O'Dea's time, Thomas Street in Catherine's day constituted a self-contained village, even a souk, its streets lined with stalls and a plethora of retail outlets – Liam Hayden remembered eight shoe shops. There were little shops like Mahers that sold covetable, new-fangled 'convenience' food: 'Anything in a packet was wonderfully exotic and therefore desirable – because Mum always cooked wonderful wholesome food. Do you remember Vesta curries? Rice in a separate bag and bits of beef in miniature squares that you reconstituted by soaking it in water? And the separate little sachet of sauce?'

Not to speak of that yummy Cadbury's Smash, all the rage and still, I see, on sale in my own local shop.

Almost opposite the distillery was a shop called Duffys 'and they were way ahead of their time. They had a waving

Santa!' You could buy your Sunday newspapers on Saturday nights outside Bakers pub, in response to the 'Oyee! Oyee!' call of the winkle-pickered Teddy Boy paper-seller and his Teddy Girl girlfriend. 'You'd be a bit afraid of the Teddy Boys, not for any reason at all, I don't remember any violence. It's just because they were a bit different.' And just as Liam Hayden was conscious that his residency in Frawleys gave him immunity from hassle in the less savoury areas around Thomas Street, Catherine felt that she, too, was part of a community that protected its own. It was a wonderful place to live, with every facility on the doorstep. 'The library was only a few steps away, as was the Pipers' Club.' The Hogans went to that venue a lot, particularly when one of the distillery workers, a well-known piper named Tommy Reck, was playing. There were folk sessions in the Lord Edward and the Castle Inn, and after the young Hogans had reached a certain age, their house became a social magnet and crash pad for pals coming in for the entertainment.

In the early seventies there was a disastrous fire in the distillery. 'It was Dad who had brought gin to Powers and it was awful for him to watch the Gin Tower go up like that. But we didn't make a big palaver out of it. "Nobody was killed", that was the mantra.'

Time marched on and the six Hogan children, adults now, dispersed. Powers was subsumed into the portfolio of the multi-brand company, Irish Distillers. The senior Hogans retired to a cottage near Brownstown Head in John's beloved Co. Waterford from which they watched Irish Distillers in its turn become a component of the giant Pernod Ricard.

The Thomas Street premises are now the National College of Art and Design. Catherine could not think of them being put to better use. 'They've planted rowan trees at the back. Dad would have loved them.'

Cow

From ten o'clock today
Till somewhere after three,
A black cow resisted arrest
In an alley off Thomas Street.

During that time
She terrorised three hundred mothers
Coming home from their sodality Mass,
Dislocated a downchute
On the church wall:
And kept a priest late
From a Legion meeting in Fairview,
Daffodils forlornly withering in his hands.

Two women had to be assisted
To the priory
And dosed with Valium and tea,
A man fell from his bike
Outside 'the Clock'
And looked for confession
For the first time in twenty years;
A meths drinker

On Power's steps
Woke in panic
To what seemed the Armageddon.

All in all
An air of carnival was achieved:
People left their work
To come and stare,
The spectators themselves
Becoming spectacle.

Someone rang the fire brigade
But they refused to come,
Unless she could be lured
On to a tree
Or put in danger
From flooding or fire;

The evening papers
Showed no concern,
Concentrating again
On stolen cars
In Sherriff Street
And the newest outbreak of hostility
In Teheran.

Padraig J. Daly

My Parks

If the Phoenix Park was the Hogans' back garden, albeit a pretty impressive one at 1,750 acres, it was my own family's most consistent destination for outings.

We picnicked in the Hollow, a miniature valley opposite the gates of Dublin Zoo. The bonuses here were that you could eat your tomato or banana sandwiches to the strains of a concert being given in the bandstand, maybe by that Army Number One crowd, and also, if the grass wasn't too wet, you were allowed roll down the hill, top to bottom, even in your good clothes. Music, it seemed, really did soothe the adults' savage breasts.

The zoo itself was not a regular destination but a very special treat. It wasn't just the price of four admission tickets that was a deterrent. There was no point in going to the zoo if you couldn't afford the extras. These included a bar of Cadbury's Fruit and Nut and a packet of monkey nuts, sold in twists of paper by the barrow dealers outside the entrance, a ride on Sarah the elephant, and on the little train pulled by Shetland ponies round the zoo's central route. It all mounted up so the zoo was reserved for birthdays or First

Communions. At least the chimps' tea party was free and I laughed along with the crowd as, dressed in funny costumes, they sat around their little table, or sometimes jumped up on it, spilling their cups. But I was half-hearted about it. Something didn't feel right.

As for Sarah, patiently carrying squads of swaying children on her back the same short route over and over again all afternoon, I was too young not to enjoy it, but I remember being upset by the cruel hook on the tip of the iron bar carried by her keeper.

In October, when mist rose from the wet grass of the park, and the deer ducked in and out of peripheral vision, we threw sticks into the branches of the huge chestnut trees in an effort to dislodge their harvest. You peeled off the horny green covering to find the conker nestled in its soft white hood, but even in the time it took you to get home its gloss had dimmed. Threaded on pieces of string, it was left on a sunny windowsill to harden.

Conker championship season, during which the object was to smash your rivals' conkers with your own, was short and brutal, certainly for me. I never even got close to being a winner, even in the preliminary rounds.

In retrospect, the Phoenix Park was a wonderful resource – it still is – and some of my happiest memories of the sixties were formed when I roamed its plains and valleys on an Arab pony named Fudgy, hired by the hour from a local livery stable. The estate was even bigger when it belonged to Hugh Tyrrell, Baron of Castleknock, who deeded it to the

Knights of St John of Jerusalem. These built a monastery on the present site of the Royal Hospital, now housing the Irish Museum of Modern Art.

When Henry VIII confiscated the monasteries in 1537, the knights lost theirs. And on the restoration of Charles II, his Irish viceroy, James Butler, Duke of Ormond, stocked it as a royal deer park for the gratification of the hunting classes. The perimeter wall, eleven kilometres long, was built in 1680 to keep out the plebs until 1745 when a later viceroy, Lord Chesterfield, threw open the entire park to the public.

When my brother and I were young, we took the park for granted. The wide steps of the Wellington Monument were for running up and down. The Furry Glen was for nature walks, the People's Gardens for snide giggling at the cut of the old folk sitting silently on the benches while our parents admired the flowerbeds. We were told how lucky we were to be able to watch polo for free so we stood respectfully at a white rail and watched the upper classes gallop up and down the scutchy field on agile ponies whose tails were tied up in a bun. We never bothered with the cricket, though.

I always admired Gough's statue and, in particular, thought his horse to be the most gorgeous depiction of an animal I had ever seen. This beautiful bronze, sculpted by the Irish artist James Foley and erected in 1880, survived numerous attempts to blow it up, including one that resulted in the loss of Gough's head and one leg of the horse – both of which were subsequently found in the Liffey. Another attempt in 1956, also bungled, gave rise to a satirical ballad:

There are strange things done from twelve to one
In the Hollow at Phaynix Park,
There's maidens mobbed and gentlemen robbed
In the bushes after dark;
But the strangest of all within human recall
Concerns the statue of Gough,
Twas a terrible fact, and a most wicked act,
For his bollix they tried to blow off!
'Neath the horse's big prick a dynamite stick
Some gallant 'hayro' did place,
For the cause of our land, with a match in his hand
Bravely the foe he did face;
Then without showing fear – and standing well clear
He expected to blow up the pair
But he nearly went crackers,
All he got was the knackers
And he made the poor stallion a mare!

On 23 July 1957, a proper job was made of it and the statue was left in ruins.

Since it was obviously such a nuisance, no attempt was made at restoration this time. It was sold off by the Office of Public Works in 1984 and is still in England, despite pleas from various quarters, particularly around the time of Dublin's reign as European City of Culture, to have it returned for display in a suitable public venue.

If it is still on anyone's agenda, I support that idea.

When our family finally achieved the Holy Grail, our own car, we used to drive the snaking hilly U-bends of the rally course on the Chapelizod side of the park, stopping for a walk at the Magazine Fort.

Built in 1735, this, too, gave rise to the derision of a satirist – Jonathan (Dean) Swift:

Now here's a proof of Irish sense,
Here Irish wit is seen,
When nothing's left that's worth defence,
We build a Magazine.

Like the Gough statue, it attracted unwanted attention because it was stuffed with explosives and ammunition, according to my father who, with relish, would explain that at one point 'subversives' (unspecified) had attempted to blow it up and had 'failed miserably'.

This was semi-accurate. There were two major infiltrations of the Magazine during the twentieth century. The first was an attempt to blow the arsenal to high heaven as a signal to all of Dublin that the 1916 Rising against the British occupiers had begun. And, in fact, two Volunteers did manage to get inside but, apparently unable to find the keys to the main stronghold within the fort, had to content themselves with a small detonation, which wasn't heard beyond the perimeter wall of the park.

The second raid achieved its aim. It took place on the day before Christmas Eve in 1939 when the substantial weaponry stored there belonged now to the Free State. This time the IRA planned well. They captured the building with relative ease and removed a huge quantity of arms and ammunition, loading them onto a fleet of lorries and trundling them through the Islandbridge Gate towards their own storage facilities. In fact, there is a story that the cargo was so heavy, it broke the axles of several lorries.

The Magazine is locked up now, and the last time I passed it I saw a doe, coat glowing in the light of the setting sun as she grazed in the long grass beside it. A jogger, pounding downhill on the roadway, granted neither animal nor fort a glance. They were just there. Like always.

Oh, to Be in Doonaree . . .

Is there is anyone in the country who has not taken an outing to one of the best-known landmarks in Dublin, Clerys in O'Connell Street?

The present premises houses the second retail emporium on this site, the first, with great humility called The Palatial Mart, also included the Imperial Hotel in its upper storeys and was opened in 1853 as one of the first purpose-built department stores in the world. It traded under various owners until 1916, when it was destroyed during the Easter Rising. The current building is based heavily on the design of Selfridges in London. It is 'listed' because of its historical and cultural significance.

The rebuild included a clock over the entrance, and of course since then several generations of Dubliners, and culchie blow-ins indeed, have traditionally set dates to meet each other 'under Clerys clock'. The tradition persists although the original clock has long since gone to meet its maker in clock heaven.

Denis Guiney, who bought Clerys in 1941 when it was in receivership – he acquired it for the extraordinarily low sum, even at that time, of a quarter of a million pounds – was a Kerryman who started his retail career in Dublin in 1921 from a store in Talbot Street. Then, not too long after he opened his doors, the place was burned down by British troops at the height of the Civil War. He was compensated, so he rebuilt, expanded, and the shop became hugely successful.

When he took over Clerys he quickly increased the staff numbers from six hundred up to almost a thousand and began trading his way successfully into profit. He was a Fianna Fáil man to the core and during his era at the helm, it was said that a man could not take off his coat in Clerys restaurant without hitting a Fianna Fáiler with its tail. As well as the restaurant, the store included a ballroom and a pub, patronised by the proprietor himself and where, by reputation, the cheapest pint in Dublin could be had.

Denis Guiney died in 1967 and from then until August 2004, when she, too, died at the age of 103, the place was run by his redoubtable second wife, Mary, whom he had married in October 1938, six months after the death of his first.

So them's the facts and the history.

By any standards, the second Mrs Guiney was a remarkable character. A pillar of the Catholic Church, she was a daily communicant, and Archbishop McQuaid himself gave permission for her late husband's anniversary Mass to be held in Clerys, an event that became an annual one. Competitive and stubborn on and off the business field, she held tightly to her controlling shares in the business, rebuffing all offers of takeover or merger. She played competitive golf until she was in her late eighties and was a formidable presence at the bridge table. Even her posthumous influence on Clerys cannot be underestimated. She and Denis had no children but she left her shares to a trust, whose beneficiaries are nieces, nephews, grand-nieces and grand-nephews and, at the time of writing, the store is still principally a Guiney family business.

Like those of most Dubs, my own memories of Clerys are legion. In 1952, I had my First Communion breakfast there; I bought my stockings and white gloves there for my Aer Lingus interview in 1962, leading to the most carefree three years of my life. I was stood up under its clock when I had contracted to go on the first 'date' I had ever agreed to, and it was during the long, long hour I waited for my swain (not!) that I perfected my lifelong technique of looking purposefully cheerful while dying inside. It was to Clerys I was directed to go when I was thinking of entering a convent in 1962 at the age of seventeen and had been sent a lengthy list of the trousseau I would need to take with me. It was particularly scary in the matter of underwear.

I remember being on the 19A bus from Ballymun, which stopped directly outside the shop, and spotting my mother, with whom I had not enjoyed an ideal early relationship. Her dark hair was sunlit and shining as she walked briskly along O'Connell Street, and my throat closed as I recognised, probably for the first time, that she was beautiful. She was beautiful and she was my mother.

Then, after the birth of my second son, Simon, when I was suffering from post-natal elation, I insisted that my husband take me and my three-day-old son directly from the hospital to see what was on offer at one of Clerys' periodic sales. Mind you, 'suffer' is definitely not the apposite verb, at least from the sufferer's point of view, to describe the surges of energy and hilarity and that brilliant, almost continuous feeling of exhilaration.

My most fascinating Clerys' times, however, were in my early childhood. Like Bernard Farrell, I was taken every year to see Clerys' Santa in his grotto, queuing, hail, rain or shine, from the side door in Sackville Place. (Some years, I got to see two Santas: of the alternatives on offer, Pyms would have been my choice – there was a rich, almost posh feeling about the Pyms Santa. Clerys' man was more 'down-home' and therefore for my family, always the first choice.) While waiting in Sackville Place, I remember being entertained by a toothless down-and-out playing 'Oh to be in Doon-a-ree' on his mouth-organ; he also hummed 'Molly Malone' through a piece of tissue fixed over a comb, while holding out his greasy cap for recompense.

Your heart was always thumping hard by the time you got to stand by Santa's knee. You promised to be a good girl, he wished you a happy Christmas, then gave you a parcel containing maybe a cut-out paper doll on which you fixed cut-out paper dresses by means of bendy shoulder-tabs. Or a smooth, slim package of multi-coloured A4 carbon paper. You inserted a sheet of this precious stuff between two ordinary white bits of paper and when you wrote on the top bit, the bottom bit came out blue, or red, or green, whatever colour you had used. This was true magic.

There were times when my mother and her friend Mrs Phelan would take me into the shop where, after our cup of tea, we would go to the floor for the actual shopping. And when one or other of them went up to the counter to pay, I would stand quietly, gazing up at the tracery of wires on which, singing like happy bees, a constellation of busy little brass cylinders moved about.

For the purposes of this volume, I searched and searched but could find nothing, human or electronic, that could lead me to the formal name of this whizzy, wires-and-cylinders cash system. I can remember every detail of the sales transaction: the woman behind the counter folded your cash and docket into a small brass cylinder, fitted this back into its holder, pulled a handle and the thing buzzed slowly along a series of overhead wires, speeding up a little on the sagging downhills, until, up, up and away, it disappeared from view into the cashier's office. I knew that because my mamma told me where it had gone. Your cylinder even turned corners at junctions and, although imagination may be coaxing memory here, I even recall that, mysteriously, one never seemed to crash into another at the junctions, but always waited politely for its fellow to pass.

The assistant wrapped your purchase while you were

waiting for your personal tube to sing back towards you with change and receipt. When it got close, it slowed down and stopped with a soft *thunk*. If the shop was busy, a bunch of cylinders might arrive at the same time, *thunkthunkthunk*, coming to rest companionably against each other. My game then was to try to pick out the one relevant to my mamma's purchase. I was so fascinated that a bus could have come through the glass doors and I wouldn't have noticed. I've always loved gadgets.

So what was the name of the system? Those who used it referred to it simply as the 'Pulleys'. Even my childhood pal Helena Buckley, who worked in the Clerys administrative offices in the early seventies, knew what I was talking about and remembered seeing it when she was a child, but couldn't help me.

She did try, though. Any use if she told me the name of the machine used in the cash office for collating receipts? 'That was called the Concometer.'

Nah. No use.

Helena, as it happens, was not all that fond of Mrs Guiney: 'You'd hold a door for her and she wouldn't even acknowledge you.' On the other hand, she couldn't speak highly enough about the way Mary Guiney's company looked after its staff. 'They were very caring. If you weren't well they'd send you home in a taxi.' She herself suffered from ill health for many years – she was an undiagnosed coeliac – and at one point the management sent her to Lourdes, with a 'nice envelope of pocket money' so she could enjoy herself while she was there.

Helena had a young colleague in the office called Marie Butler with whom she struck up a friendship, despite the age gap between them. 'She was very beautiful, always glammed up in her miniskirts.' Marie took it upon herself to mind and protect my friend when she was poorly. 'She was a very, very kind person with a heart of gold.'

At one point in 1974, an assistant on the Clerys shop floor was dismissed, allegedly having been found 'fiddling' the till. In reaction, the union organised a mass meeting to protest against the company's action and as a gesture of support for their colleague. A ballot for strike was called and a show of hands was requested.

Helena and Marie looked at one another. They didn't want to strike: 'We weren't very well off and we needed our money at the time.' Nevertheless, they felt they had no choice and reluctantly raised their hands. The ballot was carried and the strike took place.

One Friday afternoon, 17 May 1974, Marie walked up to Parnell Square to collect her strike pay from union headquarters before it closed.

She was crossing Parnell Street when a car bomb was detonated and she was killed, with thirty-three others during what have become known as the Dublin and Monaghan Bombings.

Marie Butler was twenty-one. The strike against Clerys was called off when the person on whose behalf it had been held was reinstated.

Running the Country:
The Man from Rathmines

Like Aidan Mathews, his fellow writer Ronan Sheehan was born into the 'professional' middle class and had a very similar upbringing, Donnybrook meeting Rathmines. The two met at Gonzaga College to become fast and lifelong friends. 'We are joined at the hip,' Mathews said, on hearing that his friend, too, was to contribute to this volume. I hadn't known of the connection when I contacted them separately, confirming, yet again, our by now well-established polity.

Unlike Mathews, whose presence is slight, retiring, almost owl-like, Ronan Sheehan's is imposing, even patrician. He is tall, expansive where his Gonzaga chum is contained. They must make a nice pair, should they choose to walk along the Bull Wall or Dun Laoghaire pier of a Sunday.

On the day we met in his mews house off Dartmouth Square, Ronan Sheehan had just finished filming a small role in the 'costume' TV series *The Tudors*, in which he plays the chaplain to Henry VIII – acting is among the talents in his quiver. He is a committed smoker, charming, voluble and, on the surface, open – but there is a wary watchfulness too, a bulwark against full invasion of his domain.

The wariness is not absolute, though. When, inadvertently or otherwise, a touch-paper is put to certain subjects, passion erupts throughout his long body, which uncoils to shoot venom and indignation about some societal wrong he has perceived. Alternatively, the reaction might be a loud laugh at the absurdity of the world.

His pride in his extraordinary family heritage is almost palpable. Although he maintains that families like his are common in Dublin, they are not.

 He trained as a solicitor in the office of his father, James Sheehan, but while he retains his membership of the Law Society, he does not practise; his brother, Garrett, is a judge. 'By education and upbringing you were encouraged to think you knew it all. It wasn't that the people who sent their children to school in Gonzaga were fantastically wealthy, but there were expectations of influence and ability . . .'

In this regard, he quotes a certain Father White, the prefect of studies at the college who, when he heard unruliness in a classroom, would throw open its door: '"What is the meaning of this disturbance?" And then, not waiting for a response: "Well, I'll tell you what it means. You people are supposed to be *running the country* in twenty years' time, and if you don't, who will?" And then he'd shut the door.'

Sheehan's entire body windmills at the memory. He finds it so funny he has to light another cigarette.

His contemporaries and friends all lived in good houses in good areas – Palmerston Road, in his case. Their parents and relations ran motor-cars and benefited from a good standard of income and education. Most importantly, they enjoyed status, an evanescent gift within any society.

Outside Rathmines and their other playgrounds, the tennis courts and rugby fields of Rathgar, Terenure and Donnybrook, lay Darkest Africa – and in this he echoes his friend, Mathews, although in starker, less tactful terms. 'On Sundays my Aunt Nora, who was a great tennis player, used to come along in her car and take us to the zoo. We had membership there so we went to the zoo quite a lot. My feeling as a child was that as soon as we crossed the Liffey we were in a completely different world. That it was miserable. I couldn't wait to get out of it.'

'Over there' he saw slump instead of the easy posture he was accustomed to amongst his own kind, who swung through their leafy streets with the gait of entitlement. 'The streets in the centre of Dublin were in a different condition of life altogether. I could see that people were impoverished. The Quays. Dorset Street. Gardiner Street . . .'

Ugh.

'The children in O'Connell Street were scruffy, dressed differently. They often had problems with their teeth, something you don't often see now . . .' And so, after these dispiriting Sunday visits to the zoo, the young Sheehans and their Aunt Nora hightailed it as quickly as possible to Sandymount for a consoling picnic.

That was the schoolboy view, of course. As a young adult working in his father's law office, his view softened radically, ignorance and fear of the unknown replaced with fervid empathy. 'I was interviewing young men of my age who as children were picked up for petty crimes, brought into the Children's Court, undefended, then picked up by slave dealers to go to reformatories where they were raped. That was the reality.'

The flames quieten when he thinks about how Dunnes Stores stirred growth of well-being and self-respect in the Dubliners he had derided at one point but whose cause he now ardently promotes. 'Say what you like about old Ben Dunne, but Ben Dunne clothed the people of Dublin to a respectable level. That is a serious contribution. It gave people a sense of dignity.' Ben's cheap school uniforms mattered a great deal too because 'school, not home, was the centre of your universe and uniforms give a status in society that you have to live up to'.

The bookcase in his living room is stuffed. The room's walls are covered with photographs pinned up in neat and meticulously organised sequences for 'the novel I'm trying to do now'. In it he will try to fill what he perceives as a gap in the canon of Irish literature that he says no one else, however celebrated, has attempted. 'There has not been in our fiction or drama an aesthetic representing the state.' He excepts the serial, non-mainstream work of Mannix Flynn, 'so novel it has been ignored, its premise being that you – the people, the state – are responsible for crimes against citizens.

'Dublin was well served by Mr James Joyce, and it is convention to say he was so big everyone else was minor in comparison. But Dublin was a colony in those days – those were the politics and it is very difficult for writers suddenly to come into the Free State and to produce a way of describing what it meant. Yet in my view it ought to have been done and that it hasn't has impoverished the canon. We get characters and buildings to the detriment of politics as the essence of the city.' He reels off what he means: 'I was walking down the street and I met Johnny Fortycoats and we went in and had a jar and we met Flann O'Brien and he told a couple of stories and here they are . . .'

He lights another cigarette.

In his novel, the Special Criminal Court in Green Street will be a metaphor for the state. 'A kind of rhetoric. In fictional terms this is quite simple: the institution precedes this state. By chance, I can go right back . . .'

He means by heritage, and gives a brief and partial tour of his wall of research photographs: 'That's my cousin, Margaret, beside that one of Sarah Curran. You can see how alike they are . . .'

Sarah Curran, secret fiancée of the executed patriot Robert Emmet, whose portrait hangs above those of the women, was the daughter of John Philpott Curran, a Protestant, Cork-born barrister who opposed the Act of Union, supported Catholic emancipation and defended Wolfe Tone after the Rising of 1798 – yet who disowned his daughter when he learned of her 'betrayal': falling in love with Emmet.

He has left a wonderful piece of oratory, however. It was recorded when, as Master of the Rolls, he was rendering judgement on a contested will, the beneficiaries of which were due to be 'twelve reduced gentlewomen' of the City of Waterford and the 'education of poor children'. In finding for the trustees of the testator, he said 'that the object of the bequest is to provide shelter and comfort for poor helpless females, and clothes and food and instruction for poor orphans'. Then he uttered what might stand alone as a testament to a fine and benevolent mind: 'Would to God I could see more frequent instances of such bequests. Beautiful it must be in the sight of God; beautiful in the sight of man it ought to be; to see the last moments of human life so spent in acts of gratuitous benevolence, or even of interested expiation. How can we behold such acts without regarding them as forming a claim to, as springing from, a consciousness of immortality?'

John Philpott Curran's Dublin descendant continues the magisterial tour: 'Over there is another famous cousin, John Adye Curran, who prosecuted the Invincibles.' Those patriots were a motley crew, linked to disaffected Fenians. They perpetrated the 'Phoenix Park Murders' in May 1882 when they ambushed and killed their target: Ireland's Permanent Under Secretary, Thomas Burke, because he was a 'Castle Catholic', a traitor who worked for the hated British. It was the misfortune of Burke's newly arrived boss, Lord Frederick Cavendish, to be walking with him at the time. The murderers seized this God-given opportunity and killed him too.

There are many more photographs and portraits on Ronan Sheehan's research wall, but their subjects are beyond the allotted span of our interview.

He was awarded the prestigious Rooney Prize for Literature in 1984. He is very proud of one of his non-fiction publications, *The Heart of the City*, based on a collection of photographs 'taken by a man called Brendan Walsh in the inner city'. Although he has just used it, he hates that phrase: 'It's not a Dublin phrase. It's from a Chicago socialist: if you were from an inner city you were a problem. If you're a Dublin person you are from a street or a parish.

'My mother and my Aunt Rose and my father were very proud of being Dublin people and of Dublin, but Brendan was from a Dublin Republican family. He revealed to me a city I didn't know and that my education hadn't shown me, Sheriff Street, Buckingham Street . . .'

Coupled with his education in his father's office, his adult *volte face* from childhood distaste was now complete. Now the 'other' side of his city was filled not only with squalor and children with bad teeth, but with stories and heritage as vital and important as his own. He decided to explore, and did so with the zeal of the converted. The book was published in 1988 and has been taken up by UCD and Trinity for some of their courses. The important thing for him, however, was that it was read by the people of those streets and parishes. 'To my delight, they think it's a good book.'

He now sees *The Heart of the City* as a resource for the book he has been preparing to write all his life. 'I have always had an ambition to write a really good book, a novel, about Dublin'. Despite the pooh-poohing of his literary friends – 'Go and do an English MA in Trinity' – his decision to work in his father's office was also study for that writing. 'I knew I'd learn a lot more about society by working in a law firm.'

With Neil Jordan, he was a co-founder of the Irish Writers Co-op in the 1970s; this collective published early work by its members and others such as Sebastian Barry, Desmond Hogan and Mannix Flynn. He sat behind Jordan in the National Library while both were writing. 'Neil was working on a book called *The Past*, describing a family background from the founding of the state. The mother is an Abbey actress, the father is IRA, but at the end he just stops. He concludes with *there came I,* whereas what should have happened is that the state came out of this, not the individual. I don't want to be too Olympian about it, but the ideas I express now are those I have developed over a lifetime. He should have written a companion piece or a sequel.'

At this point, I might hazard a guess that Ronan Sheehan could be seen by the literary establishment of Dublin as somewhat of a Troublesome Priest. He certainly doesn't think he has to hold back what he feels. 'No one is really engaging with the politics of the state or even portions of it. John Banville avows the politics of the place he writes about and won prizes for writing about relationships in Rosslare.

Colm Tóibín's *The Master* is a Henry Jamesian exploration of relationship. Now in that same year in County Wexford came another book called *The Ferns Report* by George Birmingham, senior counsel. It's not for me to say what Banville or Tóibín should write about, but *somebody* should be writing about Wexford.'

In this vein, he tackled John McGahern on his 'writing about farmers in Leitrim' after a talk the late author gave in UCD summer school. Afterwards, they were conversing in the famous theatre in Earlsfort Terrace where, according to Sheehan's father, who had attended there, ambassadors used to flock to hear debates of the Literary and Historical Society because Ireland's stand in the Second World War would be important. 'What about the politics of the generation you're talking about?' Ronan demanded of McGahern. 'But John wasn't getting into that. The psychology of farmers. He does that very well.'

Time for another cigarette.

'Enormous changes are occurring. Our society can now be seen as a success where once it was a failure – but we don't know how to write about it. These things were already happening within a stone's throw of where Flann O'Brien was working in the civil service. Why didn't he write about them?'

Well, Ronan Sheehan is embarking on it. Politics, societal politics, are very important, especially in Dublin families like his own within which, he says, certain matters could not contemporaneously be broached.

He was very close to his mother. She was a Becker. (Hello, polity! *That* Becker – Becker's Tea? Remember the piece about Bests? Frank O'Dea's list of North Earl Street shops?) She used to sing with the Rathmines and Rathgar Musical Society. (Hello, Kevin Hough!)

Georgina Becker was aristocratic, brought up in India with a British Army background and 'with ancestors buried in St Paul's Cathedral in London'. When Ronan himself was growing up in Rathmines, he was conscious of divisions within the family: that some traditions might not be expressed, as evidenced by the placing of two of his mother's family portraits, now hanging on his own wall, in the mud room of the family home. 'Not in any of the main rooms.' His father's side, you see, included family friendship with Arthur Griffith, so it is understandable that there might have been a frisson within the household. 'Those things are identifiable to every Irish family, but not every family has ancestors buried in St Paul's Cathedral.'

Nor does everyone's family tree include the Jesuit who accompanied his colleague, Campion, to the gibbet at Tyburn in 1581. St Edmund Campion, canonised in 1970, was a brilliant Oxford scholar and orator. He was tortured and martyred on trumped-up charges, having refused an offer of release by Queen Elizabeth herself, should he recant his faith.

If Sheehan and his mother were close, his relationship with his father was chary for a long time and he saw him only as a 'forbidding authoritarian figure. I came to realise later that he simply wasn't good at intimacy.' Sheehan Senior came from a 'bread-and-dripping' background. His own father had died when he was only four so his self-containment was understandable. 'But when I went to work with him I got to know him on his own terms. He was a wonderful lawyer, and a very good teacher. We developed a working relationship – but more than that.' It seems both sides grabbed on and worked within the safe bounds of the office, where power lines were not blurred.

James Sheehan specialised in conveyancing. In the same way that Cearbhall Ó Dálaigh encouraged love of Dublin buildings in his godson, Aidan Mathews, Sheehan's father took his son on odysseys around the city, explaining who had owned which house and when, and to whom it was sold on. 'It's a Joycean image, really.'

It was far, far more than any writer's image. It was father saying to son, 'I love you,' in the best way he knew how.

One of the fundamental things Ronan Sheehan finds interesting about Dubliners now is that relatively few people still live in the area in which they grew up; that while they think of themselves as being on the upwardly mobile escalator, most are now dispossessed.

Like many another, while he welcomes much of the city's redevelopment he disapproves of some desecrations: the loss of Wood Quay, for instance, was a tragedy, as was the widening of some old thoroughfares. 'I'm a person who believes in the economic prosperity of the city and of its citizens and I'd do a lot to ensure that citizens of Sheriff

Street and Buckingham Street have a proper standard of living. But I also believe that an integral part of the heritage of the city is its cultural integrity and if we had preserved Wood Quay we would have had an amazing feature and expression of that history.'

Like me, he mourns the trickle-down and dilution of 'the authentic Dublin accent' into a stew combining the worst of Los Angeles and Mayfair, especially among young people, 'who are influenced by movies and American TV programmes'. He still hears it, though, around the pubs of Buckingham Street: Burke's at the corner of Amiens Street, Morley's at the Summerhill end, now that he has overcome his childhood reluctance to dally or dance there.

He went so far as to travel voluntarily along Dorset Street on a day when there was a big match on in Croke Park and was *amazed* at what he saw. 'It was a carnival. People thronging into the pubs and outside the pubs and all wearing the county jerseys. There was a very welcoming feel. I could have joined in, but that would have been false. I couldn't have gone on to pretend that I'm from that world on the basis that I'm from Rathmines.'

There would have been little point either, he thinks, in his approaching one of these revellers to make common cause that one of his grandfathers was from Marlborough Street, although he left it in 1835. 'That wouldn't have gone down too well.' But the point he is making, with genuine surprise, is that *anyone* could have joined in. Even him. 'You could have been from Balubaland.'

He is not, of course. He is from Rathmines. But now that it's 'Go Buckingham Street', a passion that burns straight and true, anything is possible.

Pauline conversions, Dublin, Ireland, emergence from colonisation, complex family histories, oratory, martyrdom at Tyburn, murders in the park, Green Street as metaphor: Ronan Sheehan's planned novel is hugely ambitious. Its seedlings have been planted throughout a vast steppe, deeply matted with undergrowth. Never mind talent and skill, only someone of serious courage and iron-clad tenacity could envisage the path through the forest that will ensue. What a prospect!

Outings

These days, 'outing' means something different from what it did in Dublin forty, fifty or sixty years ago. At that time, when your father decreed that an outing was in order, it meant simply getting out of the house 'for a breath of fresh air' *en famille*, usually on Sunday after Mass and dinner.

Year round it could mean watching the planes from the back of the airport. Word would spread that Aer Lingus was getting a new one. Or that some new airline was flying in as a once-off and you had to fight for your place on the viewing balcony or in the little lay-bys thoughtfully provided by the authorities along the perimeter fence.

In September, it meant a dreary trip to the 'country', in reality quite close by, in the fields beyond Ballymun or Finglas or up near Knocksedan, where we got our feet wet in ditches and snagged the wool on the arms of our jumpers as we attempted to fill containers with wormy blackberries.

October was the time for outings to Griffith Avenue to wade through the ankle-high drifts of crackling brown leaves shed by the magnificent trees that lined it. (My own specialty was that each year I brought my roller skates and attempted to skate through them, a futile exercise as the wheels clogged within seconds. But I persisted and sometimes managed maybe twenty yards before grinding to a halt.) And if the family was flush some Saturday, there was always the possibility of the zoo and renewed acquaintance with Sarah, the elephant.

July and August meant day trips to Portmarnock in a big green bus malodorous with hot diesel, sweaty runners and loud with the shrieks of overburdened mammies trying to stop their offspring standing on the seats or pestering the conductor for ticket rolls.

Already plundering the tomato sandwiches meant for the picnic on the beach, we chuntered out through the lanes, then pulled into the parking area beside a shop hung with promises of seaside delights in the displays of beach balls and flimsy bamboo rods with circles of green fishing net attached to them.

It was there I developed my lifelong addiction to salt because I always used my pocket money to buy a packet of Star crisps, threepence, with the little blue twist of paper containing salt: you'd fish this out, open it carefully and shake it over the crisps. There was never enough, though, and only the top crisps tasted salty; the ones at the bottom tasted of wallpaper paste bound with ancient dripping.

But my introduction to the Dublin Riviera took place when my nanna, who disapproved mightily of the freedom and independence my parents granted me, took me to Dollymount Strand on the bus and held my hand as we walked gingerly across the wooden bridge, me praying I wouldn't fall through the big cracks into the water far below. The tide was out, and when we got to the strand, she spread our blanket and sat on it. Then she extracted a long rope from her huge handbag. She tied one end round my waist and, holding the other tightly, sat down. I was then allowed roam as far as I liked. All the way to the end of the rope.

I remember sitting disconsolately on the wet, hard-packed sand, watching other kids digging and running, flying kites, splashing in the distant water. I did my best, excavating little holes within the radius allowed.

We spent our allotted hour, she reeled in the rope, untied me and we went home.

The only other outing I remember with her was to a circus in the Theatre Royal. This was a rather peculiar experience because she insisted on taking me out to the toilets every time any remotely dangerous act was announced. So I missed the trapeze, high wire, knife-throwing, fire-eating and the lions – although I could hear one or two roars from behind the door of the lavatory at the back of the stalls. I was allowed to watch the plodding elephants and the placid, wide-bodied horses who cantered round and round the ring, nodding their plumes and remaining apparently unconcerned that humans were somersaulting and performing other acrobatic feats on their sturdy backs. So, I suppose it was worth at least half the entrance money.

Walking through Stained-Glass Windows

If a gumboil could boil oil
How much oil could a gumboil boil
If a gumboil could boil oil?

This charming ditty was one of our childhood chants. It was an era when poor nutrition, the price of coal and sporadic dental attention in certain areas of the city led to 'minor afflictions', which did not feel minor to the sufferers. This was when girls could be seen in school yards rinsing out their mouths with water from the cold tap in an effort to gain temporary relief from burning gums. They would surreptitiously lick swollen chil-blained fingers, or ease off their shoes under desks – hoping that these transgressions would not be spotted by eagle-eyed, cane-wielding teachers. When many children were motherless, from TB, childbirth, or simply exhaustion.

Brendan Behan is reputed to have opined that anything which moved beyond Inchicore and Dolphin's Barn was either a cow or a culchie. The consternation within his own family, who found themselves relocated to Kildare Road in Crumlin, can only be imagined.

But in search of work, droves of culchies did come to Dublin after the war years (they still do!) and secured housing alongside the locals in the new suburbs, not only in Crumlin but in Finglas on the north fringes of the city. Dermot Bolger's mother and father were among them. He feels he was lucky.

We meet in All Hallows, one of the most peaceful, bosky places in the city. Bertie is reputed to jog there; shining-haired Americans laze about on the extensive lawns while taking breaks from their theology and philosophy seminars and courses. The place has been a diocesan seminary since 1842, following which, each graduating year, squads of young men went out into Dublin and away, confident of doing God's business all over the world. Given the current poor state of vocations to the priesthood, however, the college has had to diversify.

Bearded and wearing studious-looking spectacles, Bolger, poet and novelist, fits neatly into the All Hallows ambience like the Ghost of Christian Past. As we pad towards the canteen along the polished-wood floors of a corridor, we pass photo-montages of each annual priestly graduating class. For decade after decade, the individual photos were tiny, swarming in their communal frame, but with each year of the last thirty or so, the individual snaps get larger and larger until by the 1990s you could see the creases round the eyes of these hopeful young men.

Dermot lives close by in Drumcondra with his wife, Bernie, and their two sons, but he was born in Finglas, 'in the upstairs back bedroom at 21 Finglas Park'. The Bolgers were runners into this new and hopeful suburb of Dublin, with a Co. Monaghan mother who had worked as a chambermaid in the Moira Hotel in the city, and a Wexford father who crewed on the small ships that plied in and out of Dublin port.

They moved into Finglas not as a nuclear unit but as an extended family group, occupying three houses adjacent to each other, one for Dermot's immediate family, one each for the families of his mother's brother and sister. Those houses, with 'massive back gardens', had been built, no doubt for their own flock, by the Church of Ireland, but the Irish government would not grant aid them unless Catholics were allowed to live in them too.

Since country blood ran in the veins of many of these new suburban Dubliners, they saw the green tracts as a resource and put them to proper use. 'It was a land bank of greenery. You'd open your back door and there'd be a hedgehog, or a fox . . . You woke up to the sound of hens chucking around the place. Or digging. The cutting of long hedges.'

Reverence for the soil ran deep. The father of Shane Connaughton, writing colleague and friend of both Dermot Bolger and Peter Sheridan – who told me this – cycled to and from his plot of land every weekend after work to take care of it.

So?

He was a gárda stationed in Cavan and the plot was in Finglas.

The Malones next door to the Bolgers had a hen run and

apple trees. Next door to the Malones were the McDonnells, with their plum trees and a football pitch – and, inevitably, their hens. 'We called it "Henyan Park".'

He is not romancing about the football pitch. John McDonnell had laid it out and encouraged the neighbourhood kids to use it. 'We played until eleven o'clock at night. We played in the dark.' Although Henyan's chairman could not run to floodlights, water-logging never stopped play because 'John was a technological genius. He had these massive foam things he used to soak up the water.'

Next door again were the Piggotts, whose back garden housed real horses in real stables and who were plagued by the heads of young footballers popping over their boundaries: 'Could we have our ball back, please?' Bolger is absolutely mad about football, playing it, watching it, following it, talking about it, injured by it. On the day we met he was limping, wonded on the field.

His sister, June Considine, also a novelist, has written about their bucolic, virgin suburb. She contributed to *Invisible Dublin*, a book of essays about the new Dublin settlements that her brother published under the aegis of his own Raven Arts Press, founded when he was but a pup, and expressed wonder that each family had its own front door, *used by no one else except yourself and your family.*

She, too, remembers that neighbouring roosters greeted the dawn and that many gardens contained chicken runs, with sods of turf, dug from the bog allotments on the Wicklow Mountains, stacked against the garden walls . . . and that 'difference' was tolerated and accepted: '*The Man lived in one of a row of small cottages near the school. Tall and white-haired with a bushy moustache, he would stand stooped in his doorway and suddenly begin shouting, in a shell-shocked voice, triggered off on the killing fields of Europe. "A war victim," our mothers said, touching their fingers to their heads. "He was shell-shocked during the war."*'

As the tired and huddled masses of Dublin followed the country people into Finglas, '*we accepted our disappearing countryside under the rows of houses which now widened the narrow lanes, and the new children, with their thin city faces, who filled the classrooms to overflowing . . .*'

Acceptance sea, 'ecumenism' *ní h'ea*. That was a step too far for Finglas chisellers. '*Occasionally we would descend from the lofty tones of theology to chant, "Proddy Proddy – go to hell. Ringing out the Devil's bell," and the answer would auto- matically follow: "Catty, Catty – go to Mass. Riding on the Devil's ass."*'

June's brother can chart the evolution of the village with his school moves. First there was a three-roomed prefabricated National School on Ballygall Road. Then he and his fellow pupils were moved to the cellar of St Canice's church, 'walking downstairs to the dark through the stained-glass windows', and finally, when it was ready, into the purpose-built St Canice's school.

Unfortunately, the original three-family group in the three adjacent houses did not last long because work was scarce and first the aunt's family, then the uncle's had to find employment in the car plants of Luton. At least the uncle managed to keep his family in Ireland, moving over and back across the Irish Sea as often as he could. 'He'd come home, a great big countryman from Monaghan, and he'd plant the potatoes and he'd go back to Luton; and then he'd come back and harvest them.'

The family of Dermot's aunt, however, had to give up the dream and the entire family had to emigrate, not revealing this to any of the children, including their own, in advance. 'My brother Roger remembers standing looking at them leaving in a taxi and our cousin Johnny looking out of the taxi window and waving goodbye, and neither of them knowing that emigration was afoot. Yet they did know something was wrong.'

Emigration was a very big factor. There came the day in 1967 when Dermot himself had to say goodbye to his best friend, Pat O'Hanlon.

Pat's mother had been struck by the demeanour of a group of Trinity students she had encountered in Bewley's, Westmoreland Street, with their glossy, carefree carriage and obvious expectations that 'Trinners' was a stepping-stone to success. Life for them was a peach. Her kids, she decided there and then, would go to university too.

Reality bit with its usual sneer. Her kids go to Trinity? Fat chance they could come within a mile of that sacred campus – or any other.

But Mrs O'Hanlon was a resourceful woman, and as she travelled home she was already thinking hard.

The answer was simple: the whole family should emigrate to Canada, where hard work was rewarded and where the financial barriers to third-level education, stoutly maintained against incursions from the working classes in Dublin, could be breached. So off they went.

Sounds so glib and easy. 'Off they went.' Slips like summer ice-cream down a grateful throat, sliding across the American Wakes, the severing, the long, heartbreaking goodbyes. But the ploy worked – eventually. 'They had a tough few years, but they all did well. Pat O'Hanlon now owns a championship golf course.'

Dermot's father, Roger, 'kept us in Ireland by emigrating twice a week on a steam packet' and fishing off Iceland. The symbol of that time for his son is his da's brown Travelite bag: bag in the house, Da present; no bag in the house, Da gone. 'He still uses that bag.'

Although the picture he presents is of a happy, thriving childhood, it is not complete and must be shaded with darker colours. He had a cross to bear, a debilitating and isolating stammer that exacerbated his innate shyness. 'When you have a stammer you're made to feel very stupid by your peers. You can't communicate. A stammer is a wall between you and other people. Going for a pint of milk is a nightmare. All the way there you're saying the phrase over and over to yourself so that you will be able to say it.'

And, of course, by the time you get to the shop you're so tense your tongue seizes and you can't say a word. 'The only way to get around it is to say something else and introduce the phrase on the sly.'

A speech therapist told his mother that behind the clouded communication was 'a very bright penny', but his mother never lived to see its full glory. 'She died when I was nine.'

Perhaps because this handicap forced him into an interior world, even in National School Dermot Bolger was writing poetry. He had a friend at that time called David who wanted to join the army: 'I'm going to be a soldier.'

'Well, I'm going to be a poet!' It was blurted. It seemed to come from nowhere. Certainly to the pal, who was gobsmacked: 'You can't be a poet. You'd have to go to university.'

This, they agreed, presented a problem. But despite his shyness and his stammer, young Bolger was made of strong stuff. He confided his ambition to a teacher at St Canice's, a Michael Donnelly who, astonishingly, did not disabuse him of the previously unheard-of notion that a St Canice's boy from Finglas, still under twelve, could aspire to becoming a professional poet. (Dermot Bolger's first poem was found many years later when the school was being refurbished.) 'He actually encouraged me to leave school a couple of months early', although not before he had sat the entrance exam for Beneavin College. 'Go on. Live life!'

So he left and got a job as a summer helper on an ice-cream delivery van. This van's driver, by the way, was no ordinary plodder, but an 'extreme character' who had our hero ride on the outside of the passenger door, holding on for dear life through the open window while he himself played Fangio, throwing his vehicle round bends and careering through the narrow country lanes of North Dublin, Lusk, Rush and Lough Shinny.

Somehow the helper lived. At the end of the summer, he went on to Beneavin secondary school, where he got further literary encouragement from his English teacher, a man called Hewitt. 'Of course you can be a poet,' this enlightened teacher said. 'Anyone can be a poet. All you need is a pen and paper and the use of your imagination.'

At around this time, when he was thirteen, his sisters took his stammer in hand. They sent him to the Betty Ann Norton School of Speech and Drama in Harcourt Street – and his first encounter with the middle class. 'It was a different world. I'd never come across them before. They glistened, a bit like the pope did when he came to Ireland. Very confident people.'

On his first day in the class, everyone was asked to mime making a cup of tea, pouring it into a cup, adding sugar and milk. This, you would have thought, was a fairly simple exercise. Dermot thought so anyhow and, deciding that since he was there he might as well have a proper go, stepped up to the plate and did his bit. Afterwards he thought he had done OK.

When everyone had had their turn, the class was asked to comment on each individual's performance. Dermot Bolger, they concluded, had done well. Very well, in fact, but there was one big flaw: *he had used the same spoon to stir the tea and to put in the sugar.*

'I found I did not belong among them. I didn't want to ape them, I wanted to stay on my own course.' So he survived in his own way. During improvisation classes, for instance, he acted as class clown, 'cutting loose, having the room in stitches – and then retreating back into my own world'. And to prove to himself – the only critic he cared about – that he could do it, for the entertainment of those at home he reproduced great tracts of the spoken soliloquys he had heard in class. Fluently. Without a mistake or a forgetful pause.

He might have gone to university in an era beyond Pat O'Hanlon's when it could have proved possible. But he deliberately did not, probably, although he does not say so, for the same reasons he cut his own path through the manicured shrubberies at Betty Ann Norton's.

As a young man, his determination that he would not join any 'establishment' extended to a conviction that poetry readings should not be the exclusive preserve of the gently educated classes of the southside. 'Literary Dublin could come to me in Finglas.' So early in his career as a publisher and poet he set about launching a book of poetry on his own turf. He secured a venue, a beautiful little Protestant church. He also secured a few well-known poet-luminaries who would read. It might have worked too. There was enthusiasm from and acceptance by all concerned.

He asks me to be tactful about what came next. I will. But I will reveal his mental snapshot of the unfortunate clergyman, head in hands, sitting in his church while all around him raged imbroglio. A small number of his guests, obviously fearing what faced them on the wild side of the Liffey, had 'tanked up' beforehand and were consequently emboldened vociferously to make known their feelings about specific poets and their poetry.

Bolger is vehemently *not* a 'Molly Malone' Dubliner: 'that "true Dubliner" thing is a load of bollocks. I've never felt less of a Dubliner because my great-great-grandfather didn't come from the Liberties. A city is a bastardised space, a flux of different peoples.'

His Finglas was never perfect. 'You knew the corners to avoid, what fellas to stay away from. My wife is from Donnybrook and she would walk anywhere. When we were going out first, she couldn't figure what I was doing when I'd wheel away suddenly to go in the opposite direction.' He echoes Bernard Farrell and others in lamenting the new and more vicious breed of thug. 'In those days you could talk your way out of situations.

'But Finglas was just a microcosm of Dublin. The minutiae of class was evident. Bono used to say that where he grew up he could go for a ten-minute walk in the evening and change social class five times.

'Although we were all brought up to say our address was somewhere else', as much of his literary work shows, Dermot is exceptionally proud of his birthplace and to the day he dies he will promulgate not only its early charms but its future entitlements.

And now that he deserves and enjoys public success, 'I'm still very much a working-class Dubliner, football on Friday nights. I'm deliberately holding on to that. I've continued to live my life the same way I would have when I was in Unidare, and want to continue to lead it as an ordinary working-class northsider.' To earn his early crust after leaving school, he took a job on the assembly line in that factory as a 'slugger', forcing chemical sludge through a small hole to create coatings for welding rods.

Dermot Bolger is an 'authentic', to employ a word used preposterously to describe everything from sliced white bread with a few gritty grains added, to pastiche cottages in Conn- emara holiday villages. 'You are shaped by where you're from.'

He is the real deal and so is his Finglas, five classes, divisive dual-carriageway, scarred and blasted greens and all.

St Stephen's Green

In the absence of 'massive back gardens' that could accommodate city farms, 'Let's go and feed the ducks!' was an invitation familiar to all Dublin children in my time and is still current. 'Feeding the ducks', while frequently literal, is a euphemism for a stroll in St Stephen's Green.

My own connection with the Green is that my grand-uncle, Jack Butler, was its superintendent for many years, and my mother often spoke of being taken to visit him and his family in the little gingerbread house inside the south-west corner of the park at the junction of the Green, Harcourt Street and Cuffe Street. I have never been in it, but feel as though I have. I regard it with a proprietorial eye whenever I take a short-cut across the Green, threading my way through the mitching schoolboys, students, courting couples and 'ordinary' Dubliners rambling over its lawns and along its paths.

How many know that this place was originally a swampy field of sixty acres where snipe-shooting regularly took place? Or that it was named after St Stephen's Church and Leper Hospital in Mercer Street? Or that on 24 October

1773 an unfortunate woman, a Mrs Herring, was executed there by being burned alive?

The Green remained open, with access from a laneway (currently Grafton Street) until 1663 or 1664 when Dublin Corporation fenced off twenty-seven acres as a 'green lung' for the residents of the houses to be built on the remaining thirty-three. It remained closed, to the resentment of the general populace, until in 1877 Lord Ardilaun, Sir Arthur Guinness, pushed through an Act of Parliament that decreed the space was to be opened to the public. What was more, he followed this up by putting his money where his mouth was; he paid for the entire area to be planted and landscaped.

The stream, complete with waterfall and O'Connell Bridge, is a marvel. Do those Dubliners who fling the remains of their lunch to the crowding wildfowl on Lord A's duckpond ever speculate about where it comes from or goes to? It is a diversion from the Grand Canal, a tributary if you like, piped underground from a location above Portobello Bridge, to empty back into it at Mount Street.

Did the poet Patrick Kavanagh, who recorded his birth as a poet (as opposed to a versifier) 'in or about 1955 on the banks of the canal', know this?

The Thing

We had the Chime in the Slime, the ambitious but short-lived digital Millennium Clock placed in the Liffey by a sculptor whose quantum of hope far exceeded realism. We had the Floozie in the Jacuzzi – the Smurfit Fountain, now in 'storage' in Raheny. In 1953 though, Dubliner's propensity for the renaming of public attractions and sculpture was nowhere in evidence.

In an effort to leaven the general bad mood and economic doldrums, the authorities came up with an idea to attract exiles home, at least for their holidays: a series of festivals and events known as An Tóstal. Included in Dublin Corporation's contribution was the erection on O'Connell Bridge of an artefact officially called The Bowl of Light. It contained artificial flames set in a fountain and lit from underneath. Hope would be rekindled in those who saw it, and returning exiles, even the local population, would realise there was Light at the End of the Tunnel, that it was Better to Light a Candle and that it was always Darkest Before Dawn.

In reality the 'flames' drooped in the rain or flapped in the wind that almost always howls up the Liffey from the

Irish Sea. The effect was far from captivating and not even the wags could think of an appropriate nickname for it, until the comic, Jimmy O'Dea, came up with the Tomb of the Unknown Gurrier.

Even this moved quickly into the realms of archive because after a couple of weeks some of Dublin's disaffected youth removed the Tomb from its moorings and threw it into the river.

It was replaced with a raised flowerbed, for which Dublin, still stumped, could come up with nothing better than the Thing.

The Vision

All right, if you want to know more about the Thing, or almost anything to do with Dublin, Pat Liddy, who earns his crust from the living city, past, present and future, is your man.

He is accustomed to guiding foreigners on walking tours through the lesser-known corners of Dublin as well as acquainting them with its famous landmarks. He talks, as a result, in sequential, cohesive sentences and it should be a joy to interview him. Let 'er rip. Straight transcription. Add a few links. Bob's your uncle.

It is a joy to interview him, but the subsequent difficulty for the hapless chronicler is that he has so much to say about his city, all of it making sense, that it's impossible to know what to leave out.

Not 'Dublin is still one of the most fascinating cities in the world. We can substantiate that. Our museums and art galleries house the world's greatest collection of prehistoric gold and silver and the world's second greatest – and maybe best – collection of Islamic Korans. We have the world's biggest urban park, twice the size of Central Park in New

York. Bull Island is the world's only biosphere within city limits. Everywhere is within easy reach of mountains and the sea. Howth is six hundred million years old – I could go on.'

He does. 'There are so many positive things about Dublin. As keepers of all this man-made and natural heritage, we are starting with a palette of wonder and all we have to do is to apply the colours in a nice orderly fashion so that we have a lovely picture to present to ourselves and everyone else.'

He takes a sip of his red wine. His choice of venue for the interview is the atrium of the Westin Hotel on Westmoreland Street. It's a good place to sit in quiet comfort when its glass roof is being assaulted by the monsoon firepower of a Dublin summer. Today, though, I don't mention the weather. I'd be afraid to.

He has secured a place on the ladder leading to the strongholds of some of those who hold Dublin's future in their hands – planners, developers, the City Council, businesspeople. His role, he believes, is to reveal a vision for the city then aid its realisation. There are others with vision, of course, 'but a lot of people, from government right down, will pay lip service, and when push comes to shove a lot of bureaucracy doesn't enable it. There may be a vision for Dublin now but it's not a connected vision. I'd be worried that it's just going to take too long.

'Bertie has said he'd like to see things being done quicker, but it seems that he's right when he says that at present it takes eight years for the public sector to build a hospital from the time we decide to build it to the time the first bed is occupied.

'They're talking about spending thirty-four billion euro on infrastructure in the country, most of that around or leading out of Dublin, three metros, seven more Luas lines and so forth, and that's grand. I'd add pedestrianisation – and tunnels everywhere. Forget the nonsense we had about the height of the port tunnel. We've the highest tunnel in Europe. Bertie's right there too but he seems to be a lone voice. We don't want those high trucks. They're an English institution. They're not allowed on the continent.

'We bring in a law about no five-axles going through the city and it works for a couple of weeks but now I see so many five-axles in the city they couldn't all be on permits. We're a great country for laws but we don't back them up.'

His visualisation of our future city, which, given the pace at which progress is made here I will never see, is one in which pedestrians stroll along elegant boulevards, stopping now and then at cafés or bistros, or to shop in superstores and glowing speciality niches. There is not a cigarette butt, hamburger wrapper, bottle or piece of discarded chewing-gum in sight. Everywhere is staffed by the friendly, efficient, courteous Irish, native or immigrant.

He welcomes the ten per cent of 'new Irish' now resident in the city wholeheartedly. 'I employ guides for my tours from Japan, Russia, Poland, Italy and Spain, because they are Dubliners now.

'Many Dubliners have mixed histories anyway, fighting in

the wars for the British Army, even the Cromwellian Army. One of the lovely things about history is how it revolves. A thousand years ago Dublin was a multicultural society. You had Normans and English and Irish, monks speaking to each other in Latin, and with the ships coming in and out from all over Europe, you could walk down Fishamble Street and you'd hear French, Norse, Latin, Irish, Saxon, Anglo-Saxon, Spanish . . .'

For him, the new Dublin, whatever it will become, has to be about integration, integration, integration, with 'no exclusivity', and all the little villages within the city encouraged to stay villagey: 'Sandymount people, for instance, are very proud of their maritime history. Phibsboro, Donnycarney, they're all going to be redeveloped.'

And so is Finglas. 'Finglas is one of the great messes of the sixties. It got more than its fair share of the worst architecture and something will be done there too.' Grangegorman is going to be a city up there on the northside – 'It will be a university in time.' And as for the 'village' now rising around the Point, 'that will be a serious destination. A village of 50,000 people.

We eat a few nuts – nuts, really nice nuts, come with the drinks in the Westin. We need sustenance because we're taking off now, nose to the lifting wind.

Airborne, we turn our attention to the Liffey. Specifically Dublin City Moorings, the berths beside the present Dockland offices on the North Quays. 'For a city mooring it's very cheap to tie up your boat there. We should take advantage of that. And the Khashoggi-type boats will come in with the conference centre.'

Now, the river itself is, as we all know, visibly tidal. 'If it is to become the waterway and thoroughfare it could and should be, there's only one solution. It has to be dredged, seriously dredged. It has a stony bottom and we have to go down a good few feet.'

Way, way past the shopping trolleys.

We eat a few more nuts. His faith in the future is so infectious it is irresistible. And although I feel I should insert the disclaimer that *most* of the opinions in this piece are the interviewee's own (including the one that got him into trouble about many of the famous 'bullet holes' in the GPO not being bullet holes at all), I find myself nodding furiously and throwing suggestions or opinions into the otherwise perfect sentences that encapsulate his vision. If you could bottle and sell Pat Liddy's enthusiasm for his city and her future, you would make a mint.

'We have to spend a few hundred million euro. We have to build a barrier to regulate the flow of the Liffey. A type of lock gate at Butt Bridge or even at the East Link. It could be done, but whatever way you do it, boats should be able to access Heuston Station.'

With a business partner, his next wheeze is to augment his walking tours of the city with Segway tours of the Phoenix Park, eight riders to a guide, communication on the move by microphone and headphones. 'We can form a circle at specific places, stop for a cup of coffee—'

Segways?

Large-wheeled gyroscopic scooters, powered by eye/body co-ordination and body movement as though the riders are walking. They can climb inclines, perform a 360-degree turn on a micro-dot and travel at up to 20 km. an hour. 'We led the St Patrick's Day parade with eight of them, but so efficiently that the parade fell behind us. We're trying to get them recognised as alternative transport.'

In this venture, for which they now have a licence, he hopes that individuals will participate for the fun experience, but that 'corporates' could also be enticed to organise team building exercises around them. At present there is no legislation in place to cover the use of Segways on public highways or footpaths – is it a bird? Is it a plane? – but at the time of writing there are only a few in Ireland, possibly because each one costs a fortune – about six thousand euro.

Liddy's own fortunes have varied. He started his career in Aer Lingus when it was on O'Connell Street: 'It's hard to imagine now that you could park your car on O'Connell Street or even stop outside Clerys to pick up a parcel.' After some years, however, his line drawings of Dublin streets and landmarks were attracting favourable attention, not least in the *Irish Times*, where they were regularly reproduced with extended captions. So he ditched the airline for art, setting forth bravely on a full-time career as an illustrator, columnist and author of his own books about Dublin. And latterly, of course, as über-guide with his own tour company.

Books can make money for their authors and publishers

but a lot of them – a *lot* – don't. Pat Liddy was not immune to this flux but remained undaunted. He was convinced ('convinced' meaning *convinced*) that not only was he doing what he was destined to do, but that he should share his limitless passion for Dublin, past, present and future, with everyone. (And 'everyone', as you must already have gathered, is *everyone*. Everyone on the planet.)

He hands me one of his latest babies, a smashing little colour tourist map of the city, eight million of which have been printed for distribution by the tourist authorities. He has even got it into the pockets of the gárdaí: 'The police are regarded as a friendly presence in this city. I've succeeded in getting them to accept that they are part of the welcoming committee for tourists. They're the only police force in the world that can give a tourist a map.'

But, of course, it won't stop there. 'I'm hoping I can take it to the next level, bring them on courses where I show them things they might not have spotted, the heritage of the beats they are on, for example, the buildings and so forth.

'This is a fantastic city for walking. The perception that a lot of tourists have before they come in is that it's the Book of Kells, St Patrick's Cathedral, the pubs in Temple Bar and Guinness's – and that's it. They have it mapped out already. "Hidden corners? There couldn't be!" So it's got to be put out there that Dublin is actually worth a city visit.'

We're soaring. 'This vision thing is not new. If you go back to the seventeenth century there was official vision in the sense that the viceroy, the Duke of Ormond, tackled

Dublin's first developer, Humphrey Jervis. "Yes, we're delighted that you want to build all along the north side of the quays but we don't like the way you're planning to build the houses, backing right up to the river as a convenient sewer. I want you to build away from the river and leave eighty feet from the edge of the river and the front doors of the houses with a boulevard running between them. To use the river as a focal point for good urban living.""

This Duke of Ormond, the man who laid out the Phoenix Park, 'stroked' Lord Essex, the lord lieutenant, for support in other areas too. Essex's surname was Capel, so Capel Street and Essex Bridge, the first to link the north and south quays, were born.

Mind you, development was hazardous even then, according to Liddy; at one stage Jervis ended up in debtor's prison.

Lord Mountjoy was another visionary, whose plan was to create a Royal Circus for Dublin – like the one in Bath but on a bigger scale. Its centre was to be the site where the Mater Hospital now stands. Radiating from it, like spokes on a wheel, there would be a series of fashionable avenues. His plan was interrupted when, answering the call of duty to join his yeoman regiment, he travelled to New Ross in 1798 and died from a musket ball to the head.

The Pembroke family's vision of a Grand City was at least partly fulfilled on the southside, where they built from Fitzwilliam Square to Sandymount and Ballsbridge. 'OK, they were going to make money by selling the properties but, crucially, they had a pivotal role in deciding what should be built, how, and how it should be laid out. Any damage done to Ballsbridge and that area has been done since the 1960s when we lost the integrity of all these areas.

'That continues to happen. It's all individualistic, towers replacing hotels. There's no one sitting down to decide on the overall plan about what's to happen in different parts of Dublin.' As for the great Georgian terraces of which we are now so proud, 'in the eighteenth century you had a mixed bag of developers who were not all that worried about the vision thing but were building for profit.'

We are losing height. 'A lot of those terraces were jerry-built, put up quickly and adorned internally with nice plasterwork and so on for flogging to some unsuspecting MP or bishop or someone.'

More height lost – because the state of public transport in Dublin is his biggest bugbear. And it is at your peril that you mention the lack of integrated and extended ticketing: 'Our governments have been notorious in neglecting or even opposing what has worked in other countries. For some reason our ministers and civil servants travelling to cities like Brussels and Strasbourg must always have been picked up in limousines and so forth and must never have been in a tram. They have no idea how useful trams are and would be.

'The vision that might have been produced in the twentieth century about making Dublin into a transport-viable city would have destroyed much of the medieval core of the city and communities. And so it didn't happen, but in a sense it has been happening by stealth.' (Clanbrassil Street, anyone? High Street? The Finglas dual-carriageway?)

These are arguments and plans, and arguments about plans, that have been well-rehearsed in Dublin and national forums and are ongoing, soon again coming to a newspaper or radio show near you. So, no point in going too deeply into them here.

Anyhow, hooray! We're off again, up, up and away with the Business Improvement Districts scheme with which Liddy is involved. 'You select a district – or several – within a city. You start with one and make money available to improve the facilities and ambience for the public.

'This has been very successful in many Canadian, Australian and American cities that were in trouble, including New York. We'd be one of the first in Europe. And this time we got our friends and our enemies onto the same committee, architectural organisations, An Taisce, the business groups, the car parks, engineers, Trinity – people who might normally be in conflict. If you bring them in at the beginning and sweat out the conflicts between you, then you present a united front with the plan. The government couldn't resist it.'

So it's a 'go', with the first plebiscite of business owners and operators to take place in late 2007, covering premises in an area south/north from the top of Grafton Street to Parnell Street and east/west from Amiens Street to Capel Street. If there is a 51 per cent vote in favour, the plan swings into action.

The downside for businesses is that their rates go up by

a 'small' percentage, but in Liddy's view the advantages of the scheme far outweigh this. It is win-win for business, for his beloved city, and with huge spin-offs for tourism.

The way it works is that the extra money collected, 'maybe four or five million', is ring-fenced, its use and disbursement supervised by an elected committee representing the ratepayers themselves and the city council. It is spent solely on improvements, in particular on supplementing the regular cleaning schedule. A footpath or roadway is cleaned or a bin emptied whenever necessary or desirable and not just by timetable. There will be 'hospitality officers' on the streets to act as the eyes and ears of the district. They will look out for litter, over-full bins, a patch of footpath soiled with vomit or urine and have it sorted within minutes. They will also keep an eye open for tourists and others in need or trouble.

For keyholders, the payback for having to fork out extra rates in this Utopia is that with more security and CCTV, more and improved street furniture, including 'nice' seats, extra signage about heritage and landmarks, ('not just signs about how to get out of the area'), punters will throng. They will stay longer, spend more money, business will boom and property values go up.

'Although both were done in conjunction, this is what cleaned up New York more than zero tolerance.' With the cleaning up – both literal and metaphorical – of parks and streets, people felt safer ('someone is looking after me') and came more often to the city for events and concerts, or simply to linger and enjoy the streetscape.

For Pat Liddy, putting a portion of the rates back into the hands of the people who actually pay them in order to improve their area is a no-brainer. 'Whenever the government gives extra money to the council, it goes into benchmarking and wages, not services.'

The nuts are gone now. We scrape the bottom of the dish for the powdery residue. 'A problem that has beset Dublin right through to the 1990s is that national and local governments were run by rural people. The capital appeared to be getting everything and this was an embarrassment to those in high places who were originally from outside the city. But since half the population now lives in the greater Dublin area, I think that by now politicians are easier in their minds that something must be done about our problems.'

'Yet 'doing something about our problems' is not the same as having a vision. 'The government now has Green partners who are insisting there should be an executive for Dublin. With four councils, you're not getting minds to meet. There are a lot of organisational situations that keep us back from the vision but if the public are aware of what they need, want and deserve, and what they should have, they have to make their voices heard.

'Up to recently, though, the only people you had living in the city centre were people in corporation flats, fine people but who had no political clout.' However, his theory is that with 'richer people now resident in Dublin 1 and 2, it should make a dent in political thinking'.

He is all in favour – that's a *million* per cent – of a

minister for Dublin, one 'who would have the courage and the ability to sort out what seems perfectly obvious to everyone'. Someone 'who would not merely add another layer of bureaucracy', thereby slowing down even further the pace to which we hapless citizens have had to become accustomed.

Thump! Although there is still tons to talk about, we've landed.

'A Dublin dictatorship for ten years would be the ideal solution to get things done.'

Note to spokespeople for Dublin City Council: as I have already outlined, *most* of Pat Liddy's opinions are his own.

And the streets shall again be filled with the sounds of children playing thereof
–Ezekiel

Pat Liddy's vision for safe and pleasant streets in Dublin city includes safe suburbs. For adults and children. Here it might be mentioned that some of our pastimes of the fifties were not all that safe: placing pennies or nails on railway tracks to make discs and screwdriver blades; scutting: hanging by our fingertips, like bedraggled bunting, off the backs of moving lorries.

From the age of eight, I lived in a rented house on Fairfield Road in Glasnevin with a ready-made social group on my doorstep. We had a great time and cost our parents virtually nothing except the sixpence a week most of us got as pocket money on a Saturday morning. This would buy one bar of Cadbury's Fruit and Nut, or thirty-six Honeybee toffees, or eighteen Nancy Balls (tooth-breaking aniseed), six liquorice strings, six Fizz Bags or a bagful of eye-watering Cough-No-Mores, black as coal and probably carved directly from eucalyptus trees. Not for the faint-hearted.

Most of us chose combinations of the above. Choosing was the big deal and we probably drove the poor lady shopkeeper mad in our local newsagent's at the corner of Botanic and Mobhi Roads as we dithered, changing our minds from minute to minute.

Nobody splurged on the chocolate. We picked it up, drooled over it, but always put it back.

Eight years later, on the day I got my first wages of two whole pounds per week by spending my summer holidays stuffing Leaving and Inter Cert results into envelopes at the Department of Education in Talbot Street, a bar of Fruit and Nut was the first item I bought. Ever since, I have judged comparative affluence by this power of mine and I still get a kick out of knowing that I can *actually go to a shop and buy a bar of chocolate.*

For play, our street gang had many free options. If we had lost our marbles down the shores, if every hula-hoop on the road had split and the last skipping-rope was being used to tie shut some da's shed door, there was a whole lot we could still do.

We could join hands in a circle and sing:

Wallflowers, wallflowers
Growing up so high;
We're all pretty maidens
That never want to die;
Especially Deirdre Purcell
She is the only One;

> Oh, fie, for shame
> Oh, fie, for shame
> Turn your back against the game.

Still moving with the circle, Deirdre, turning her back, held hands backwards. The game continued until everyone was named, had turned and was dancing backwards with their shoulders virtually dislocating.

If we could not lay hands on even a burst football to play Donkey, we could resort to walking the walls. We simply got up on any suitable one and walked along it tightrope-style.

There was a daring variation of this one, in which a second person 'walked the wall' coming towards you on a direct collision course: either both managed to get round one another or failed and fell off. This happened to me on the wall round the Glasnevin branch of the Bank of Ireland. I fell very heavily and, a few hours later, found myself in the Bon Secours hospital having an emergency operation to deal with a burst appendix.

If we were out of chalk, or if the piggy (usually an empty Nugget polish tin) was missing so we couldn't play Beds – Hopscotch in other areas – two of us could hold a secret consultation to choose two passwords, one each. Then we made an arch by raising our joined hands above our heads. All the others marched round us, passing under the arch, each in turn:

> Here's the robbers passing by,
> Passing by,

Passing by,
Here's the robbers passing by,
My fair lady.
What did the robbers do to you,
Do to you,
Do to you?
What did the robbers do to you?
My fair lady.
Stole my watch and stole my chain,
Stole my chain,
Stole my chain,
Stole my watch and stole my chain,
My fair lady – *Wham*!

We brought down the arch, trapping the girl who was underneath it. She was asked to choose one of the words. Then she stood behind the girl of her choice, holding on to her hips. This game continued until there was no one left to go under the arch. Whichever of the two had more hangers-on won.

In retrospect, I think the chants were the real purpose of many of these games. Some were even politico-contemporary, like this one for skipping:

Vote, vote, vote for de Valera!
In comes Cost'llo at the door-i-o
Cost'llo is the one
That'll have a bit of fun
And we don't want de Valera any more-i-o!

Then there was Dusky Bluebells. We would form a circle, holding hands at head height. One girl was chosen to slalom through the raised hands:

> In and out go the dusky bluebells,
> In and out go the dusky bluebells,
> In and out go the dusky bluebells,
> We are the masters,
> Taparappa rappa rapper
> On my shoulder,
> Tapparappa rappa rapper
> On my shoulder,
> Tapparappa rappa rapper
> On my shoulder,
> You are the chosen!

With this, the walking girl would stop and put her hand on the shoulder of the girl in front of whom she found herself; this girl would leave the circle and join her in the middle, again, conga-style, grasping her by the hips. The circle would re-form round the two and the chant would begin again. It continued until there was just one girl remaining to be chosen but it rarely got that far, because by the time there were only two left making the circle, the conga line had no room to move and the game frequently ended in collapse and a tangle of giggling bodies and limbs on the footpath.

We knew not what we were commemorating. The folklorist Eilis Brady wrote a fascinating book about Dublin children's traditional street games. We sang her title, *All In!*

All In! (The Game Is Broke Up!) at the tops of our voices to summon the last straggler back to the den when we got fed up looking for him or her during Hide and Seek.

In her book, Ms Brady catalogues the bluebells game as 'Darky Bluebells' and reports that, in response to publication, she received a communication from an academic based in southern Alabama explaining that it depicts the buying and selling of African slaves.

Bulldog was two lines of kids holding hands firmly and facing each other as though preparing to perform the Walls of Limerick. There was a solemn coin toss to determine which of the two lines was first to 'go'. This 'go' consisted of the winning line running bald-headed at top speed towards the other, crashing into it in an effort to breach it. It was dangerous, there were injuries, but it was also exciting, mainly because it was body contact, boys against girls. However, we girls were aged seven to ten or thereabouts, many of us bigger and heavier than our opponents, so we were more than a match for them.

We needed nothing, no toys, money, prizes or chauffeurs, for any of the games we played on Fairfield and Daneswell Roads. We had a great time and kept ourselves occupied without wraparound sound systems, designer jeans, branded trainers, X-Boxes or YouTube. We weren't driven to playgroups or horse-riding classes – our families had no cars anyhow. While I was exceptional in that my Auntie Nellie took me on outings every Saturday, I had no difficulty filling my social diary for the other six days of the week!

I know I have painted a nostalgic picture here, and that in general we were unaware of our parents' lives. I know that in being warmly housed and properly fed, as a family we were relatively privileged and that 'rare oul' times' in Dublin during the first three-quarters of the twentieth century were a mighty struggle for a huge number, even a majority, of Dubliners; there is little dignity in poverty and neither repression nor hypocrisy should be celebrated.

I accept that times have changed and that there are new evils and dangers out there, leading parents to schedule their children's (supervised) time and to be afraid every time they say 'goodbye' at the front door. But there were always evils and dangers and deprivations in Dublin and it would be impossibly naïve to believe they can be totally eliminated from the streets and estates of a modern democratic city.

It was so different for us. During the long summer holidays, we were entirely free from adults' ken for days and weeks on end. Our mothers decanted us into the streets outside our houses immediately after breakfast and did not expect to see us except for brief spells around mealtimes or for emergency help with a grazed knee. Every Holy Day off school was a day when, after Mass, we were ordered simply to 'go out and play' and we did, on roads and paths of rough concrete for Jacks – where you threw up five pebbles, to be caught and/or picked-up in various ways – or Beds or skipping, and in gutters just made for marbles.

If we got fed up being 'out to play' or we 'weren't

speaking' to half the road, those of us still communicating could call for neighbours' babies: 'Can we wheel your baby out in the pram, missus?'

The mothers were only too glad to hand over their offspring and so we solemnly wheeled the baby up and down the road, sat it up, tied its bonnet, took the bonnet off again, put down the pram hood, put it up again, discussed whether the baby was too hot or too cold, shook the elasticated chain of plastic rattlers tied from side to side of the pram hood to entertain it, and at the first whimper, wheeled it back to its mother.

In the absence of bouncy castles, we used our skipping-ropes to swing on lamp-posts. If someone was lucky enough to get a tennis racquet for Christmas or a birthday, we spent hours taking turns to serve the ball against the nearest gable – until we were chased away by the irate householder trying to listen to the news on the wireless inside.

And if all else failed, we sat on walls and plotted the setting up of secret societies such as we had read about in *School Friend* or *Girl's Crystal,* or planned kerbside jumble sales with our own broken 'stuff' as loss leaders and our mothers' discarded handbags as the jewels of our display.

I can't remember ever being bored. And if boredom threatened, there was always the library and a book.

Street life for children can never again be the same as ours was and with wealth we have lost some sense of community. Not all, and only because we hide behind our plasma screens. And heavens to Betsy, look at what we've gained!

What should be celebrated is the resilience and spirit of our city and citizens from every walk of life and in every quarter, poor or prosperous. We did have fun, you know. Real, honest to God *fun*. We can have that again. Can't we?

Come on now, all together. With actions:

Teddy Bear, teddy bear
Tip the ground,
Teddy bear, teddy bear,
Twirl around,
Teddy bear, teddy bear,
Show your shoe,
Teddy bear, teddy bear,
That will do.
Teddy bear, teddy bear,
Go up the stairs,
Teddy bear, teddy bear,
Say your prayers,
Teddy bear, teddy bear,
Put out the light,
Teddy bear, teddy bear,
Say goodnight!

And so goodnight. Here's to us!

Acknowledgements

It goes without saying that the first people I should thank most sincerely are those who so willingly gave their time to me for interview – Frank O'Dea, Larry Gogan, Kevin Hough, Geraldine Plunkett, Helena Buckley, Patricia and Paddy Hanlon, Les and Pat Coleman, Karen Erwin, Geraldine Kelly, Liam Hayden, Catherine Hogan, Miss Anne Kelly, Dermot Bolger, Ronan Sheehan, Bernard Farrell and Aidan Mathews. Dublin, as Aidan Mathews says so memorably, is an Aristotelian polity where you can always find someone who knows someone who knows someone else. In that context, I'd like to thank Peter Sheridan, not only for his interview, but for seeming to know everyone in his beloved city and for making introductions. Similarly, Pat Liddy was generous not only with his time but with his superb line drawings.

Particular thanks to them all for being so tolerant of my repeated follow-up phone calls and my cajoling and relentless pursuit of their precious personal photographs. Thanks to my brother, Declan – that powerhouse of research – and to his wife, Mary, both of whom paved pathways to interviews, as did Suzi Guiney from Michael Guiney's in North Earl Street and also Carol and Roger Cronin.

Thanks so much to the author June Considine, and poet Padraig J Daly, for permission to quote from their work, and to Turtle Bunbury for unearthing that bawdy ballad about the Gough Statue in the Phoenix Park. For factual details, thanks to Maria Brennan from Clerys, to the staff of Trinity College Library and to Michael Talty of the RTÉ Reference Library.

I'd like also to thank the numerous authors and publishers of the books about Dublin I read as background while writing this one. There are too many to chronicle here but, in particular, I would like to convey respects to all those who contributed essays to *Invisible Dublin* (Raven Arts Press); to Phil O'Keefe for *Standing at the Crossroads* (Brandon); to Des Geraghty for *Luke Kelly, a Memoir*, to Douglas Bennett for *A Dublin Anthology*; to Frederick O'Dwyer for *Lost Dublin*; to Eamonn Mac Thomáis for *Janey Mac me Shirt is Black* – and to RTÉ and Veritas for permission to quote from Aidan Mathews's book, *In the Poorer Quarters*.

A very special acknowledgement must go to the work of the late Eilis Brady (*All In All In* published by Comhairle Bhéaloideas Éireann) because, to my great relief, it confirmed that my own street-game memory banks are still intact.

As ever, I thank all at Hodder Headline Ireland, Breda Purdue, Ciara Considine, Ruth Shern, Ciara Doorley and Peter McNulty – and indeed all at Headline UK too – for their kindness and ready support.

I think the designer and picture researcher of this book, Sinéad McKenna, deserves a very special mention.

Finally, profound gratitude to Kevin, Adrian and Simon – and to all my dear and faithful friends. You know how I feel about you, I hope (but if you don't, please send a SAE – postal orders acceptable!)

Permissions Acknowledgements

The author and publisher would like to thank the following for kind permission to reproduce images:

National Library of Ireland: Nelson's Pillar, Moore St, Communion, Sandymount Strand.

G.A. Duncan: Iveagh Market, North Circular Road, at Phibsboro, Princess Grace.

Fáilte Ireland: Crystal ballroom, Ha'penny bridge, Dublin airport, Christchurch.

Getty Images: JFK visit, Williams and MacLiammoir.

Corbis: Cresham in Flames, Eucharistic Congress.

Magnum Photos: Horse and cart © Erich Hartmann

Irish Times: Maureen Potter, Rolling Stones concert.

Broadway Restaurant: Broadway Cafe.

Clerys archive: Clery's.

Pat Liddy: Dublin Castle line drawing

Every effort has been made to fulfil requirements with regard to reproducing copyright material. The author and publisher will be glad to rectify any omissions at the earliest opportunity.